The New
Book
of Plots

The New Book of Plots

"Niemi's *New Book of Plots* is an incredible resource for teachers of written or oral expression. As an added bonus, his book is a perfect fit for teaching to core curriculae in language arts at the high-school level."

–Mary Hamilton, storyteller and author

"How I wish Loren Niemi's *New Book of Plots* had been available to me when I was teaching high-school English in Evanston. His insights are so well expressed and so clearly communicated. I predict it will become a standard for generations of story writers and tellers."

**–Syd Lieberman, Golden Apple
recipient for excellence in teaching**

The New Book of Plots

Constructing Engaging Narratives for Oral and Written Storytelling

Loren Niemi

PARKHURST
BROTHERS,
INC., PUBLISHERS

LITTLE ROCK

www.parkhurstbrothers.com
Parkhurst Brothers books are distributed to the trade through the Chicago Distribution Center, and may be ordered through Ingram Book Company, Baker & Taylor, Follett Library Resources and other book industry wholesalers. To order from Chicago's Chicago Distribution Center, phone 1-800-621-2736 or send a fax to 800-621-8476. Copies of this and other Parkhurst Brothers Inc., Publishers titles are available to organizations and corporations for purchase in quantity by contacting Special Sales Department at our home office location, listed on our web site. Manuscript submission guidelines for this publishing company are available at our web site.

Printed in the United States of America
First Edition, 2012
2012 2013 2014 2015 2016 2017 2018   12 11 10 9 8 7 6 5 4 3 2 1
Library of Congress CIP Data:

[to come]

ISBN: Trade Paperback   978-1-935166-63-4   [10 digit: 1-935166-63-8]
ISBN: E-book   978-1-935166-64-1   [10-digit: 1-935166-64-6]

Cover and page design: Harvill-Ross Studios Ltd.
Acquired for Parkhurst Brothers Inc., Publishers by: Ted Parkhurst
Editor: Stephen Ursery

102012

ACKNOWLEDGMENTS

I wish to thank Tim Herwig, for his years of friendship and for reading and offering commentaries on every version of this text. I also owe my gratitude to storytellers Nancy Donoval, Elizabeth Ellis, Kevin Kling, Antonio Sacre, and Megan Wells, who encouraged me to move the transformative experience of the plot workshops into print.

For all those who have done the work,
who have showed me the way through this book.

CONTENTS

INTRODUCTION
Some Observations 11
Who Is This Book For? 13
Some Notes about the Examples 14

CHAPTER ONE
Stories 101. 17
Why We Tell Stories 17
Creating Stories 20
Make It Your Own! 22

CHAPTER TWO
Good Bones 25
The Journey of the Hero. 25
The Usefulness of the Formula 32
Exercises 34

CHAPTER THREE
The Beating Heart 37
Constructing the Story's Arc 37
Story: *The Rake* 38
Exercises 43

CHAPTER FOUR
The Plot Forms. 45

CHAPTER FIVE
Tradition or Habit? 47
The Straight-Narrative Plot 47
Story: *The Knife* 49
Exercises 54

CHAPTER SIX
Pleasant Detours 57
The Digressive Plot. 57
Story: *Smoking* 63
Exercises 70

CHAPTER SEVEN

In Plain Sight 73
The Revelation Plot. 73
Story: *David* 74
Jokes as Revelations 78
Exercises 80

CHAPTER EIGHT

The Mirror 81
The Reversal Plot. 81
Story: *The Rabbit*. 85
Exercises 88

CHAPTER NINE

Full Circle. 91
Circular Plot, Variation One: Flashback. 91
Story: *Pablito Bueno* 93
Circular Plot, Variation Two: String of Pearls. 97
Story: *Making Chili (a)*. 98
Story: *Making Chili (b)*. 101
Exercises 106

CHAPTER TEN

Making a List. 109
The List Plot 109
Some Things I Know. 110
Story: *Sauna Cycle* 114
Exercises 119

CHAPTER ELEVEN

Fall Back. 121
The Regression Plot 121
Story: *Sleeping with Her Ghost* 125
Structuring the Transitions 129
Exercises 131

CHAPTER TWELVE

Two Trains Running 133
The Parallel Plot 133
Story: *Music Lessons* 134
Exercises 141

CHAPTER THIRTEEN

As I Was Saying 143
The Metaframed Plot 143
Story: *Moby Dick Tonight!* 146
Exercises 159

CHAPTER FOURTEEN

Other Considerations 161
Which Plot to Use? 161
In the World of Story 162
Questions to Ask 163
Story: *A Roll of the Dice* 165

CHAPTER FIFTEEN

Happily Ever After 169

APPENDIX A

Some Additional Exercises 171
A Matrix for Plotting Hero Stories 171
A Life Matrix 174
Keys to Childhood 177
Exercises for Developing Detail 179
Postcard Exercises 180

APPENDIX B

Notes on the Stories 182

BIBLIOGRAPHY OF REFERENCED TEXTS 185

RECOMMENDED READING 188

INTRODUCTION: SOME OBSERVATIONS

By profession, I am a storyteller. I am fortunate that my chosen occupation not only provides a source of income but also is my life's joyous work. The fact is, I have been a storyteller from childhood, although, contrary to the definition put forth by some academic folklorists, I am not passing along tales told to me by my family or that I took in from one particular culture.

My family did not tell stories in any formal sense. Listening to traditional or folk stories was not a regular part of my childhood, nor was I was raised hearing tales of Northern Minnesota logging camps at my grandmother's knee. My paternal grandmother spoke Finnish, a language I still have not mastered, and whatever stories she had to tell about her days of cooking in those rough-and-tumble camps were clenched as tightly between her teeth as the sugar cube through which she was fond of sucking black coffee. My grandfather, who had been a miner and a lumberjack before becoming a dairy farmer, died soon after I was born. The same is true for the grandfather on my mother's side. My mother's adopted mother was, in her own words, a no-nonsense woman who did not believe in "fairy tales."

No, stories were not told to me, but I absorbed them from the interaction of the adults around me. They were tales of illness, accidents, and work told by my aunts and uncles to each other, and children were not the intended audience. Even now, my parents' histories are sketchy and incomplete. As was the case with many children of immigrants who survived the Depression and World War II, they were focused on the future, not the past.

Furthermore, while growing up, I bounced in and out of several cultures. My parents were professionals—my mother a nurse, my father a corporate manager—and we moved every time my father got a promotion. I was born into the industrial and mixed-ethnic communities of Minnesota's Iron Range. Then we moved to the New Mexico of the 1950s—equal parts Spanish, Native American, and Cold War-era U.S. military in its cultural worldview. I spent my junior-high years among the rough kids of Buffalo steelworkers, and went to high school in a heavily Catholic suburb dominated by a culture of cars, JFK, and, later, the Beatles. Always the outsider, I intuitively observed local culture and listened for the playground stories whose retelling would help me find my way in.

Like many of my fellow Baby Boomers, my most frequent exposure to stories was through television. My fairy tales were fractured, the classics as interpreted by Bullwinkle and Rocky. My morality plays came through the tragedies of *Gunsmoke* and *The Twilight Zone*, or the comedies of Lucy and the Beaver. While the stories were entertaining, I was aware of a kind of "sameness" about them. In the world television offered, the good guys wore white hats, father knew best, and any problem could be resolved after a commercial.

Even as a child, I wanted something more. Theater, movies, books, music: I took them all in as often as I could, learning what kind of stories each could tell. Some mediums were more satisfying than others, but all lacked the intimacy and fluidity that I now recognize is central to the live, oral storytelling experience. From my perspective, the call to tell stories was not the embrace of a tradition or culture. It was an accident, a gift of Fate or Grace in spite of environment and heredity.

In my publicity materials, I say that I began as a child fibber, but soon discovered that I was less interested in telling lies than I was in improving the truth. More than just being a nice turn of phrase, this notion goes to the core of what I believe storytelling is about. Storytelling is the transmission of experience and imagination. Its primary expression was and is through the spoken word. It also is manifest in written and modern media forms, but in the history of human development, writing is really quite new and the moving image, celluloid or digital, but a blink in the course of human history.

Oral storytelling is the most basic of human activities. It recounts experience and gives voice to internal thoughts and feelings. In its traditional forms, storytelling is simultaneously entertainment, education, and transformational enchantment. Storytelling always has been the primary means of articulating our fundamental core values, of describing who we are as individuals and peoples, and of confirming our perceptions of what it means to be human. It shapes the chaos of the ever-changing world and speaks to what is "right" and "true."

Who Is This Book For?

In the space of the thirty-some years I have called myself a storyteller, the balance of what I tell has shifted from children's stories and traditional folk and fairy tales told in schools, churches, and community centers to stories drawn directly from my own experiences. But I also understand that by adapting and re-imagining traditional folk and fairy tale material, you can provide a point of entry for contemporary listeners to experience, as psychologist Bruno Bettelheim has suggested in his book *The Uses of Enchantment*, the continuing power of the old stories to speak to the imagination and heart.

Wanting to make a connection between the older stories and our existential circumstance, I sought to re-interpret folk and fairy tales by placing them in a more contemporary context. The confusing Black Forest of the Brothers Grimm became the crowded shopping mall. Rapunzel's mother sought a more familiar drug than the painkilling herbs of the witch's garden. I also created stories that were in the style of the older folk and fairy tales. One featured a lowly cucumber plant that, after consuming radioactive water and junk-food compost, became the glowing, green Godzilla of pickles. Another featured a boy named Jack, who found fame and fortune racing inner-city cockroaches.

In creating and performing original stories and reimagined folk tales, as well as teaching stories to students of all ages, it has become clear to me that *how* we tell the story, as much as *why*, is at the very heart of the art. By "how," I do not mean how we use voice and gesture, etc., but how we organize stories to get across their meanings to an audience.

There are two central facts at the heart of the oral story. The first is that it begins when the teller begins and ends when the teller ends it, though I could argue that it actually ends when the audience dismisses it. This is fundamentally different from the written story, where a reader can go back and read the same words again. With the spoken word, we are *in the moment*. Even if we could ask the teller to go back and say something again, the very act of asking would alter the way in which the information is conveyed to us. This leads directly to the second basic fact: the act of telling is an expression of the relationship of the teller to the audience. We always tell to someone, even if it is to ourselves. It is incumbent upon us to recognize that the choice we make about how we tell a story to a given audience is as much about our understanding of who that audience is as it is about what we are saying to the audience.

It is this crucial understanding of how the narrative is shaped and the choices we make as tellers to share a particular version of a story with a particular audience that I wish to explore with you. Whether we are working with a live audience in performance or with an imagined one while typing away on our laptops, the creation of compelling fiction and non-fiction begins with how to frame the story.

This book is for storytellers and would-be storytellers, whether you call yourself a writer, minister, politician, journalist, lawyer, teacher, therapist, or street-corner b.s.'er. Whatever the name, the benefit you derive from the application of this material to your creative process will come from understanding how narrative is shaped and making conscious decisions about shaping that narrative content. This book was developed in workshops and classes I've conducted with storytellers and writers since 1986. In the course of those years, this teaching practice has refined my thinking and improved my ability to help participants discover new approaches to creating powerful, authentic, and entertaining stories.

Much of what I say will be framed around the creation of stories as oral performance, but the concepts and exercises I suggest apply to written material as well. Whether the stories are oral or written, this book is about three things: the choice of an appropriate narrative form to provide the story's structure, the choice of an appropriate point of view and timeframe to support the story's emotional arc, and how those choices help or hinder the transmission of the meaning of the story to an audience.

Some Notes about the Examples

In the pages that follow, I illustrate the specific plot forms with examples from the stories I tell. This allows me to share with you my process for creating stories and the specific choices I have made using the plot form being described. By looking at how I have shaped a particular story and its meaning to me, I can assist you in thinking about your own approach to the creation process. As a caution, I do not mean to offend anyone but must acknowledge that many of the stories I tell are about adult subject matter for adult audiences. These examples are copyrighted material, and while I offer them for your pleasure, they are not to be told, reprinted, or recorded in any form without my express written permission.

Here is the confession I must make that marks me as an oral teller: while the basic plots forms of these examples remain intact from one telling to the next, the details—the pacing, sometimes even the fundamental thrust of the material as comedy or tragedy—are adjusted to the needs of the moment and my relationship to the audience. To give you some sense of how I shaped this material, I also have included, in the Appendices, background information about the examples, including notes on their development and telling.

I encourage you to read the examples out loud. It is in telling that stories live and breathe. They are changelings, shifting shape in response to the specifics of the time and place. One of the complaints I have heard from writers and readers over the years is that written texts are too dense, too abstract, and don't sound right when read out loud. For a number of years I taught courses for the Loft, a Minneapolis writing center, on "reading as performance." The hardest lesson for the writers who took the course to learn was that the spoken word is intimately connected with breath. To read your written text as if it mattered, to have it be engaging, a writer must find a way to reconcile what they have put on the page with their own breathing. An audience wants to hear the words coming from the body, not the head.

Remember, my concern is to help you create oral or written stories of your own, and, as such, the examples I have chosen should be taken with a grain of salt. You may not like a particular story, or you may think that it does not quite do what it is being asked to do. I do not consider these stories to be fixed or immutable. In some cases, I do not even consider them finished, but works in progress. They represent the choices I made at the time of this writing. If you asked me to tell one, you would not get word for word what appears on the page. If you asked me to write another version of these stories, it would reflect whatever choices I would make at that time, understanding what I do about myself as a creator of narratives and you as a reader.

I encourage you to enjoy this meditation on narrative and use it. Explore these variations of plot for yourself. Leap in. Make lots of stories, and test different versions of those stories through the mechanism of one plot form or another. In the end, you will arrive at the right forms for your stories.

CHAPTER ONE

STORIES 101

"As storytellers, we are concerned not alone with amusement, or with education, or with distraction; nor is it enough to give pleasure. We are concerned with letting a single stream of light pass through us as through one facet of a gem or prism that there may be revealed some aspect of the spirit, some beauty and truth that lies hidden within the world and humankind."
Ruth Sawyer

For those of you who already have a familiarity with storytelling, you might want to skip this chapter and proceed directly to the next one, where I discuss perhaps the most fundamental story type. If you are unfamiliar or want a short refresher course that provides some background and basic understanding of the "what" and "why" of storytelling, read on.

Why We Tell Stories

No matter how primitive or sophisticated the culture, no matter what forms of media and technology are available, human beings will use every available tool to tell stories. Not only do we tell stories, but five particular kinds of stories—myths, hero tales, trickster tales, jokes, and ghost stories—are found in every culture. The act of telling stories, and telling these kinds of stories in particular, is crucial to the creation of human culture for four reasons:

- Stories utilize the whole brain.
- Stories create external memory.
- Stories connect people to one another.
- Stories satisfy our need for meaning through ritual activity.

Stories Utilize the Whole Brain

While often presented as entertainment, stories represent one of mankind's oldest and most successful teaching techniques. Both crafting and listening to stories promote the development of both sides of the brain—the side of logic, organization, and pattern recognition, as well as the side of intuition and imagination.

Stories provide a complex and subtle learning process that stimulates both our intellectual and emotional development. They allow us to enter a multitude of times and places, to experience trouble and triumph, and to learn valuable personal lessons. Through them, we identify desirable behaviors and discourage those that harm the community.

Storytelling also promotes language development. Language provides the meaning to the world. This is the fundamental notion of "name it and claim it" as the world *is* defined by language. It is through the human brain's ability to recognize connections and create meanings via pattern recognition—the sounds we call words, the actions they stand for and our understanding of each—that we learn what is our world. Without a word for it, it does not exist for us. Our responses to the raw stream of sense data are merged into a manageable whole held together by the glue of language. "Mother," "father," "milk," and "shoe," for example, came to have specific meanings based upon our integration of actions, symbols, and emotional signifiers. We use stories to bind these symbols and emotional data bits into a manageable whole. As adults, we take this process for granted, failing to remember what a marvelous and fortunate accomplishment this really is.

Stories Create External Memory

What separates us from other species? Language? There are studies that suggest many species—from bees to whales—have complex language systems. Tool-making? Other studies indicate that most primates have tool-crafting capacities. Our stories? Now here is something to consider. Until we succeed in translating other animals' languages and collecting whatever stories they might tell, it appears that storytelling is one of the crucial distinctions we can make between ourselves and other species. In fact, it is our creation of story, of an "external memory" that does not die with the individual but is passed on from one generation to the next, that has made us a successful and versatile species.

The use of stories gives us a tremendous advantage in accumulating survival information. They tell us what to eat, where and how to hunt, how to build shelter. Stories tell us who we are and where we come from. We can learn from those who have gone before us by means of stories.

Let us look at the five kinds of stories that appear in every culture. Myths tell us how the world and our specific culture came to be. They are the unquestioned truth, the frame that we see the world through. Whether it is Genesis or the Monkey King, myths are about beginnings and the "why" of the world. Hero stories tell us what is expected, how to behave, what we value and celebrate. They speak of brave deeds done and treasures won. Trickster tales stand in opposition to the heroic, telling us what happens when we screw up. Jokes remind us of our flawed human condition and are a way to make sport of accident and bad luck. Ghost stories, which might be more properly called "spiritual stories," confront the problem of death and provide us with reassuring or disturbing answers to the fundamental question "what happens after we die?"

Each of these story types provides us with a repository of shared intelligence, a collective memory of human experience that remains independent of any individual.

Stories Connect People

Each party in the storytelling act—the teller and the audience— gives and receives information. It is this interactive nature of oral storytelling that makes it a fundamental and highly successful mode of communication that has served humans from our earliest beginnings to the present.

Whether we are sharing the history and customs of the larger community or the intimate tales of family and friends, the very act of storytelling serves as a powerful source of identification and bonding. It is this process that we use to make strangers comfortable and to express who we are and where we come from. Stories strengthen our kinship with friends and family. The act of sharing narratives can build trust as we see we have had similar experiences and feelings. It is through the telling of jokes and humorous tales that we release tension and in ghost stories that we create a safe space for the expression of fear. It is in this shared world of stories that we discover our common humanity.

Stories Satisfy Our Need for Ritual Activity

The process of storytelling satisfies our need for ritual activity. The tradition of formula beginnings and endings—whether it is "once upon a time" or "happily ever after"—serves to mark storytelling as special, as a moment of intimacy unrestrained by the conventions of logic or order.

Human beings not only make storytelling a ritual experience in and of itself, but they also use stories to enhance other ritual celebrations, such as holidays or the changing of seasons. From the pueblo Corn Dance to Thanksgiving, from Passover to Christmas, our common ritual celebrations are anchored in stories.

Rituals work in concert with our private and shared public stories to mark the geography of human culture. What is family, neighborhood, community, and country but a heady gestalt of annual events, shared iconic imagery, and oft-told stories?

Creating Stories

Whatever their type or purpose, stories are not handed down from on high. They begin with an individual's experience or imagination and are expressed in a chosen way. All stories are created, so let's begin to look at how that happens. The fundamental characteristics of a story are that it is intended, it is shaped, and it has a meaning.

A Story Is Intended

The moment you decide to convey a specific communication containing experiential or imaginative content for a specific audience, you are creating a story, whether the audience is your mother when she asks, "Where have you been?" or the 500 eager faces at the motivational seminar who want to know how to sell, sell, sell. If your communication is not intended, it might be perceived as incoherent babbling or random utterance, but it is not a story. Human beings tend to ignore or be actively hostile to those kinds of communications. In our modern culture, we also tend to medicate individuals who are prone to these unintended communications.

A Story Is Chosen and Shaped

In the instant you decide to tell a story, you must then choose how to tell it. The story the teller wants to share must be put into a form and language that is appropriate to the audience and the situation in which the communication is shared.

A well-told story engages audience members by inviting them into its world. We can ask people in the audience to experience another world that may be very different from the one they live in, or we can ask them to understand in new ways the world with which they are already familiar. The most successful stories not only create a sense of time and place, but provide or reinforce emotional connections between the audience and the teller. I'll provide greater detail on how to do this in Chapter Fourteen, which is called "Other Considerations."

A Story Has a Meaning

Whether the teller is sure of the story's meaning or not, the very process of telling it to an audience will imply that there is one. Ideally, the teller knows what the story means, at least to him or her, and makes specific choices to help the audience understand that meaning.

This is a point worth exploring. The meaning of a story is highly personalized. In fact, it can be said that every story actually has three meanings.

The first is the meaning the story holds for the teller. How successful you are at telling or writing the story often is determined by how well you understand what the story means to you and how you choose to express that meaning. If you don't know what the story is about, how can your audience know what the story is about? More to the point: Why are you telling it?

The second meaning is the one the audience hears or reads when exposed to the story for the first time. This may be quite different from the one you intended to convey. This meaning will be conditioned by many factors you have no control over: the environment the story is received in, the audience's emotional state, or something as unknowable as what audience members ate or did before they heard or read the story. Frankly, there is little a creator of a narrative can do if the audience is thinking about something else or, as is often the case, is emotionally adrift, responding to some past joy or sorrow suggested by the tale. The truth is we all listen to a story through the filter of our past experience.

The third meaning is the one that audience members ascribe to the story over time, after the story has been heard or read. This meaning is developed as audience members continue to think about the story through the prism of their experiences. This meaning is one in which the relationship is entirely between the audience and the story.

By paying close attention to your understanding of a story, your intention in telling it, the choices of plot structure and detailing that you present, you can attempt to achieve congruence between the three meanings of the story.

Make It Your Own!

As a storyteller, my first obligation is to myself, to make a story my own by clarifying what it means to me. This applies to stories we hear from someone else or ones that we create. This can be a difficult task, particularly when the story deals with a deeply personal matter. Once I've decided what its meaning is, I can make conscious choices about how I want to tell it, how to use plot structure and detail to bring an audience into the story's world.

But you should never consider your work with a story done. It is human nature to enshrine material the way it was presented to us or the way we created it. We can be particularly stubborn about the stories we create: Why should we change the precious words we have brought into the world? This is unfortunate. Good writers go through multiple drafts of a story. However, that process often is one of refining style or trimming, and not a process of reframing the fundamental way a story is told.

A story that is part of an oral tradition is meant to be performed, and all performed stories change at least to some extent with each telling. There is no way around that fact. A story breathes and shifts its weight around. It grows and shrinks as the situation demands. Even its intended meaning can change as the teller's experience and understanding of the world and human relationships change. As Walter Ong points out in his book *Orality and Literacy*, "Narrative originality lodges not in making up new stories but in managing a particular interaction with this audience. At every telling the story has to be introduced uniquely to a unique situation, for in oral cultures an audience must be brought to respond, often vigorously."

Whether you're retelling an old fairy tale or a story that you brought into the world, you can't see your words and style of presentation as immutable. You have to be ready to adapt as situations demand.

Now that you have a sense of why we tell stories, let's look a fundamental story type to begin the process of thinking about how you can shape and craft your stories.

CHAPTER TWO

GOOD BONES

"The beginning storyteller would do well to turn to folk tales, stories that have been passed down through word of mouth and polished over centuries of telling. They begin simply, come to the point, ending swiftly and conclusively. They are full of action, and the action is carried forward by the main characters. There are no unnecessary words, but only the right ones to convey the beauty, the mood, the atmosphere of the tale."

Augusta Baker

What is a plot? That is the fundamental question of this book. For our purposes, the plot, or the "narrative" as it is often called, is what happens in a story and, more importantly, how that sequence of events is organized. A typical story begins, something happens, and the story ends. Having said that, I can immediately think of exceptions, of stories in which nothing happens, and I wonder if they are without plot, or if the narrative path is not composed of action, but of something else: emotion, implied action, ennui? But even in a story where "nothing" happens, the writer needs to decide where to begin the story and where to end it. So let's set aside a philosophical argument of whether something must happen for a story to have a plot and work on the assumption that if you want to create a story, a plot is a handy way to organize the journey from start to finish.

The Journey of the Hero

Before we look at the various ways to arrange a narrative, I think it is important to understand the sequence of events contained in a fundamental story type: the journey of the hero. This story usually is presented using a straight-narrative plot form, which we will discuss in detail in Chapter Five, but it also can be organized with any of the other plot forms examined later in this book. You have almost certainly encountered this story type many times, but by looking at it in detail now, you will see how you can craft your own stories using this formula.

Joseph Campbell, in his book *The Hero with a Thousand Faces*, describes the essential core of the great myths and folk stories as a journey of transformation. He believes it is the fundamental story type, hot-wired into the depths of our individual and collective unconscious, central to our gestalt of what life is about. From Gilgamesh to Odysseus returning home from the Trojan War, from Kurosawa's *Seven Samurai* to *Star Wars*, the journey of discovery— the journey of the hero—is repeated in every age and culture.

You begin as one thing and end as another. You start in one place and find yourself compelled to make a journey, whether by choice or chance. In the process, you discover your true nature, your strengths, your weaknesses, your capacity to change. You have had an adventure and are better off for it. The heroic journey usually contains these five elemental steps:

- Invitation
- Exchange
- Challenge
- Triumph
- Return

This is the basic sequence of events of innumerable folk tales, myths, and news accounts around the world. As Campbell points out, it is always a story of separation and discovery, loss and gain, triumph and return. In Western culture, the journey of the hero often spells out our expectations of what is means to be a "good" man or woman. It demonstrates a code of honor that runs straight from Beowulf to John Wayne to Bruce Willis' *Die Hard* cop. It is such a fundamental approach to ordering a story that it deserves to be examined in some detail.

The Invitation

In this part of the story, the hero or heroine gets a call to adventure or decides to leave home to do great deeds or win a prize. It may be the youngest child wanting to make his or her way in the world. It may be the man or woman who must answer a question or heal a wound and sets out on a journey to accomplish that task. He or she might go willingly like Odysseus to fight the Trojan War and return home after many hardships. The person might depart accidentally like Dorothy in *The Wizard of Oz* or reluctantly like Jonah when he was called to be a prophet and set off to sea to avoid it.

In every case, at the very moment the invitation is issued, the process of transformation begins. Refusal is not possible because the cosmic wheels have been set in motion and the story of how the hero meets the challenge of living has begun. He or she may go alone or with companions, but go he or she must.

You may consider framing a story on the journey-of-the-hero model, so let me ask you a series of questions that will apply to either a rewriting of a traditional story or to a wholly personal tale. How do you craft the invitation in your story? What is the action that sets the story in motion? Is it based on opportunity or discontent? Is it accidental or deliberate? Is the invitation delivered at the moment the world is turned upside down, or does the invitation come before the radical disruption of comfort and surety? These are questions to ponder.

The Exchange

As the hero travels along, he or she meets someone. Often it is an old man or woman, but sometimes an animal or someone in trouble. Whomever the hero meets will ask for help performing a task. Bruno Bettelheim, Carl Jung, and many other practitioners of the therapeutic arts make much of this meeting. As Bettelheim points out, this exchange "provides assurance that the child will receive help in his endeavors in the outside world, and that eventual success will reward his sustained efforts." Jung says this moment represents the meeting with the "Other," a spiritual or psychological mentor who breaks the bonds of childhood and guides the transition to adulthood. It is a seemingly innocuous act that marks the hero as worthy. From this unexpected encounter with its deceptively simple challenge, the journey moves from an external to an internal focus.

In his book *Iron John*, Robert Bly describes such an encounter as a form of initiation in which the hero's "accepting an initiatory task is more important than succeeding or failing at it." The essential feature of initiation ceremonies is the testing of the candidate's ability and worthiness to move to a new stage of life, such as adulthood or membership in a clan. When the hero or heroine is asked to complete what seems to be an ordinary or senseless task, he or she demonstrates mettle. The task is done willingly and with a generosity of spirit.

In fairy tales, this task is the prelude to the hero receiving the help he or she needs to complete the journey. When the hero does what has been asked, a reward that is essential to the journey's ultimate success is offered in return. This may be directions, advice, an offer of help or companionship, the answer to a riddle or question, a magic object, or magic words. Often the hero does not know he or she will need this aid, or, in many cases, the hero does not know how to make use of it, but accepts it as a valued gift and proceeds on his or her way.

While crafting a personal story using the journey-of-the-hero model, ask yourself the following questions: Whom have you met along the way? Who are your mentors or helpers? Who has called you to a small task that was the beginning of an important relationship? Who has offered you advice, directions, or given you tools for success on your journey? What did you receive? Did you know how useful it was, or was that discovered at another point in the journey?

A Series of Challenges

The hero or heroine then faces a number of challenges that must be overcome, each one being more difficult than the one before it or testing a different aspect of his or her character. How many challenges does the hero usually face? One theory is that the number of challenges is based on the "core number" of a cultural tradition. When you look at the Western tradition, both European and American folk stories use three as a core number. Three wishes. Three bears. Three pigs. In numerous folk tales, there are three brothers or sisters, and it is the third one—the youngest, the weakest, the slow one—that is fated to be the hero. With three as the core number, there would be three challenges, and in story after story, there are.

As an aside, you can see how deeply we have embedded three in our worldview when you look at how it permeates our basic belief of such things as time (past, present, future), religion (Father, Son, and Holy Spirit in Christian tradition, or Virgin, Mother, and Crone in the feminist pantheon), or even our literary points of view (first person, second person, and third person). Not every culture has the same core number. Native American tradition, for example, often uses four—the four colors, the four directions, the four seasons. Chinese folk tales often use two as a core number, and feature the concept of Yin and Yang: one thing is in tension with another, but between the two of them, there is harmony.

Another approach to determining the nature of the challenges is to think about the challenges as a progression from external to internal. For our purpose, let's use the number three as symbolic of that progression. In *Rumpelstiltskin*, as an example, the heroine barters with the "ugly little man" three times. The first time, she offers him a locket, a clearly external object; the second time, a ring (symbolic of marriage and intimacy); and her third offer consists of something internal and completely personal: the promise of her first-born child. With each promise, the stakes are raised, and success or failure becomes more important.

In this kind of a progression, the role of the challenges the hero faces is to demonstrate his or her ability to master various aspects of the self, to integrate what is learned, what is felt, and what is essentially spiritual. Whatever the number of challenges, each will represent greater risk, and accomplishing them will demonstrate the worthiness of the hero.

Think about the many challenges you have faced. What would be symbolic of your coming to understand and function in a world beset with chaos and competing interests? Is it money, work, sexuality, courage, or faith that measures our true worth? How would you sort and group the challenges you've met? Which ones raised the stakes? What was at risk? What would be an appropriate progression from external to internal challenges?

Triumph

All this leads to the deciding event in which the hero or heroine accomplishes what he or she has set out to do, whether it is to find the treasure, answer the question, slay the dragon, or win the hand of the beloved. What often happens—and here again, Carl Jung, James Hillman, and other interpreters of tales stress the psychological importance of this act—is that the hero triumphs as a result of his or her own inner resources. While the hero may have used the magic words, objects, or promises of help that were offered, the external aids are not the reason the hero succeeds. In the end, it is the hero or heroine's own courage and resourcefulness that matters. The triumph is giving the inner self an external expression in word or deed.

I often have mixed feelings about our cultural predilection to use violent confrontations as the defining moment of triumph. When I look at special effects-heavy movies and television shows, the relentless barrage of bullets and blood gets in the way of understanding the actual transformation that occurs. Bruce Willis, in the first *Die Hard* film, has to summon both his courage and his cunning to triumph, but by the third installment of the series, for all his quips, he seems to have learned nothing new or lasting. In the best stories, the triumph is a moment of reflection and even loss. In *Beowulf*, as an example, the hero king's confrontation with the dragon leads to his death even while it models the obligation of true leadership and inspires his nephew, Wigstaff, to rush to Beowulf's side to offer assistance in finally overcoming the beast.

When you are crafting a heroic journey, what is the moment of triumph? What will you offer as a description of that success? Will it be a sudden and decisive event? Will it be quieter, a moment of understanding that you have changed or the world has changed for you in the process? Will the victory be sweet or bittersweet? How we choose to frame this moment says as much about the nature of the journey—whether it is a fire journey of passion or a water journey of grief—as it does about the one making it.

The Return

Having accomplished the task and been transformed, the hero or heroine returns to where he or she started from. This act of completion is necessary, for even though the hero makes an individual journey, the journey begins and, for the sake of balance, should end in relationship to the community or culture left behind. If the heroic journey is, as Robert Bly says, one of initiation into our roles as authentic men and women, then the hero cannot be recognized as an adult without returning to the community from which the child emerged. In returning as an adult, the hero can now make a contribution to the community, whereas before that person had to be cared for by the community. At the end of the original *Star Wars* trilogy, Luke stands side by side with his sister, Leia, and his best friend, Han Solo. He knows who he is, what his relationship to the others is, and is recognized as the hero he has become.

The return is the completion of a cycle, the righting of the world that was turned upside down. We really cannot afford to skip or discount this portion of the journey. Taking the time to portray the return provides both an emotional balance and a sense of closure to the journey. In most stories, the hero or heroine is recognized as such upon his or her return and is able to claim the promised rewards, whether it be the hand of a beloved, the right to rule, or the ability to live "happily ever after."

In some stories, however, the hero or heroine is not recognized or acknowledged, which usually leads to further adventures or acts as a linkage to another story. For many of us, life is a series of journeys, one after another through every stage of living. Part of being an adult is to recognize and learn from one journey in order to better understand and travel through the next.

Since all stories are fictions in the sense that we have to make choices about where we will begin and end our tale, it might be helpful to think about ending your own journey in the traditional way, with a triumphant return to a world made right, at least for the moment. If you are creating your hero's journey from the messy stuff of your own life, you may not see such an end to your story or might be tempted to deny the lessons learned. But suppose that you can. How will you celebrate your return? How are you recognized and acknowledged? What reward do you claim, and what contribution do you offer the community?

As an aside, I would remind you that while you may be the hero in your story, you are not necessarily the hero in someone else's story. In another person's journey, you may be the one who is met, the sidekick or mentor. Worse, you might be the opposition, the antagonist that must be overcome in another's story.

To really understand the complexity and interaction of all the roles that are simultaneously being played out, take a moment to consider how you would be described in someone else's journey: Did you choose that role or is it circumstantial? Do you want that role or can you change it? Can you tell the other person's story? How does your role in someone else's journey inform your own?

The Usefulness of the Formula

For creators of oral or written material, the power of the hero's-journey formula is that when a story is structured along these lines, it takes on a deeply rooted familiarity. It gives us a useful frame to see and shape material from the chaos of everyday living. This approach also gives us tremendous freedom to experiment. While the most common version of the hero's journey is done as a straight narrative, any of the plot forms in this book can be used to illustrate the essential sequence of events. Knowing what the formula is, we can create variations or play with the conventions if it suits our narrative. When audience members recognize the heroic formula of invitation, challenge, triumph, and return, they can—at least on an unconscious level—sit back and enjoy the twists and turns of the journey.

For the skeptical reader who says that your journey is not "heroic" because things do not change, or you do not see how or where you will succeed, I would say, "Try it. You might like it." Even when you are cast in the role of the helper or the opposition in someone else's story, my experience tells me that it is often worthwhile to use this formula. By shaping personal material through the lens of the hero's journey, even when we are not clear at the onset of how the formula will be expressed, we have a way to make decisions using a powerful framework. Why not consciously choose the role of the hero who is capable of transformation and triumph, and see how the life we live is, in fact, a quest for love, honor, or authenticity?

On one level, this is the function of therapy: to let us sort through our story and, in the process, understand that our life is a journey of transformation. The heroic journey may then be thought of as the primal blueprint from which human beings have created countless stories to illustrate the ways one can live an authentic life and the rewards attendant upon doing so.

Take a moment to examine any number of stories you know and see how universally this formula is applied. We can see the invitation in the voice calling to Moses from the burning bush or the exchange of the cow for magic beans in *Jack and the Beanstalk*. For Luke Skywalker, the heroic journey teaches him how to use the force within himself before confronting Darth Vader, the missing father. In Homer's *Odyssey*, it takes years for the hero to learn to shut up so he can recognize the truth when he hears it on his return home from the Trojan War. For Spalding Gray, it took a single afternoon on a beach to recognize the transitory nature of the perfect moment in *Swimming to Cambodia*. Each story is one of search and discovery, of transformation and triumph, of departure and return. The heroic journey remains a story that can entertain audiences of many cultures and ages.

Exercises

1. We'll begin by creating a story in the style of a traditional folk or fairy tale. Take two sets of blank three-by-five cards. You'll need at least five cards in each set. One set will be for the description of the journey and the other for descriptions of the world in which that journey takes place. You can use the journey cards to identify the plot and the world cards to provide details about the different characters and circumstances of the plot. By filling in both sets of cards, you can create the skeleton of the story.

On the first card in the journey set, write what the invitation is. What happens to begin the hero's travels? You can do it as a few words or as a drawing of some sort—anything that will help bring a time, place, and action to mind. On the set of world cards, begin by making some notes on the first card about your hero or heroine. How old is he or she? What does the character look like? What skills, knowledge, and values does the character have? Where does he or she live?

On the second journey card, describe the exchange. Whom does the hero or heroine meet? What happens? What does the hero receive? On the second world card, make some notes about the helper. Is the helper human, animal, or spirit? What does the helper look like? Is the relationship to the hero or heroine a one-time encounter, or will the helper go along or meet the hero or heroine at other points in the journey?

On the third journey card, put what the first challenge is. Is it physical, mental, or emotional? What is at stake for the hero or heroine? What will be gained or lost with this challenge? How will it be accomplished? Repeat this process on a different card for each challenge. If there are three challenges, you will need to use three cards.

On the third world card, identify who else is in involved in this challenge. Is it someone who is opposed to the hero or heroine's success? Is the character a rival? A villain? Is the character a human, animal, or spirit? What does the character do? Why does it matter to the character? Repeat this on a different card for each challenge you've identified in the journey set, even if it involves the same person, animal, or spirit. As an example, in *Jack and the Beanstalk*, the Giant opposes Jack in each successive challenge. But what you want to note is the what, why, or how of the successive challenges.

After the challenge cards, write on a journey card what the triumph is. What does the hero or heroine do? How does he or she achieve success? Is the triumph a physical, mental, or emotional one? What is the reward for that success? Is that reward given in a ceremony or in some other way? On the corresponding world card, describe who recognizes or rewards the triumph. Is it the helper or the opposition? If it is the opposition, why or how has that character changed?

On the last journey card, note where the hero or heroine returns to and how the character is greeted. Is it happily ever after or the beginning of another story? How or what has changed in the world when the hero or heroine returns? Why does it matter? On the last world card, note to whom the hero or heroine returns. How has the world changed? What is the relationship of the hero or heroine to those people, animals, spirits, family, or community?

Now, using the cards as a "map," write or tell that story.

2. Repeat this process using an event and people from your own life to create a personal version of the hero's journey. As a helpful hint, don't try to cover the whole of your life. Begin by looking at a small piece—a day, a week, a particular series of actions or events—that has made a difference in who you are. Use as many cards as you need to craft the five steps of the journey.

3. Since we are always the hero or heroine of our own story but not necessarily in someone else's story, repeat this process and place yourself in the role of the helper. To whom have you provided assistance, good advice, or given something that helped that person be successful? How does it feel to play that role for someone else? What reward do you get from helping?

4. Place yourself in role of the opposition. Why are you opposing the hero? How is that opposition expressed, and why are you defeated? Is it a weakness or fault of yours? What lesson is learned from defeat? How does it feel?

Once again, use the cards as prompts to create a complete story.

CHAPTER THREE

THE BEATING HEART

"And mind you, emotions are among the toughest things
in the world to create out of whole cloth; it is easier to
manufacture seven facts than one emotion."
Mark Twain

Before I examine the various plot forms in detail, I want to talk about something that is a part of every story: the emotional arc. If the plot is how we get from the beginning to the end of the story, the emotional arc is how we feel as we make that journey. Much of the success of a story will depend on how a story's plot and the use of descriptive detail support the emotional arc you want the audience to experience.

To be specific, there are three emotional arcs present in a story. As mentioned, there is the arc of the audience hearing or reading the story. What does the audience feel about the story, the characters in the story, or themselves as the narrative unfolds? As an example, in a story where the intention is to frighten the audience, its emotional arc should be one of increasing apprehension leading to the moment when a scream is the only satisfying release.

There also is the arc of the principal character or characters in the story. What do they feel at various points as they make the journey from start to finish? Finally, there is the arc of the narrator. Who tells the story is important, as is how it is told. The narrator may or may not be a character in the story. Is the narrator sympathetic to the situation or contemptuous? Does he or she build intimacy and trust with the reader or listener? Is the narrator reliable, or should the audience be skeptical? The emotional arcs of the characters and narrator in turn influence the audience's response.

As storytellers, we should be aware that all three are present and that they offer us opportunities and decisions aplenty.

Constructing the Story's Arc

The term "arc" may be misleading. You may think of it as a

version of a bell curve or a rainbow shining majestically from one end to another. It is often described as a rising line that reaches a climax and then descends as the story finishes, but it is usually more complicated than that. The best image might be one of a roller coaster that rises and falls often—the roller coaster slows down, speeds up, and by turns reassures, thrills, or frightens its passengers.

As I said in the discussion of why we tell stories, a story may mean different things to the teller and the audience. Even so, we want the audience to feel that the story in some way rings true, no matter how unfamiliar the material may be. To do so, you must construct both the plot and the emotional arc to resonate as "true" to the audience members' experiences and expectations. You can ask them to trust you with unfamiliar material, but the greater the stretch for them, the more carefully you must build the coherence between the narrative and the emotional arc.

This is difficult to do. As a story creator, you have to make a judgment about what is required to tell the story you want to tell and what will most likely elicit the feelings you want. So, you craft the story as carefully and completely as you can. You do not know how the audience will receive it. Given the range of life experiences in any group of people, there will be a mixed response no matter what decisions you make. Some will get what you are doing. Some won't.

Let me give an example of a story from my repertoire in which the plot and descriptive details have been consciously crafted to generate a certain emotional arc:

The Rake

It was one of those golden October days, and I remember it like this: I was eight, maybe nine years old. I had gone to Tommy Smith's house to play. The air was full of the smell of leaves burning and the slow, dizzy circles of red or orange or yellow leaves falling through the warm afternoon light. Tommy's older brother was slowly raking leaves into big piles. Tommy and I were chasing each other around the yard the way kids do, jumping in the piles, throwing handfuls of crunchy leaves into the air. His brother would tell us to knock it off, but we knew he didn't really mean it because he'd rake the pile we had just scattered together and step aside again.

He stopped raking when his girlfriend came over to visit. I don't remember her name, but I remember she was pretty, sitting on the porch steps wearing a pink sweater. He forgot about raking, forgot about us. Tommy and I weren't much interested in what they were doing until the moment when his brother took the rake and heaved it into the air, balancing the handle on his chin, the metal tines reaching for the sky like he was going to rake clouds. His head was back, his arms outstretched. He was stepping back, leaning forward and back, trying to keep the rake upright when it happened.

For the first time in my life, I felt time shift, felt the moment become as thick as honey. Time slowed down. My awareness expanded to take in every detail of the yard: the clouds, the trees shedding their color, the handle of the rake sliding off his chin and slowly rising up like it was weightless. The head of the rake — its thick, gray metal dark against the blue sky — turned around as if it had just noticed gravity. The brother stood there watching it happen. We all stood there watching.

When the rake hit him in the forehead, there was a small sound, a crunching sound. Time snapped back into place, and the brother fell to the ground, face down on top of the rake.

The girlfriend began screaming. The brother was screaming. The door flew open, and Tommy's mother was there. She took one look, ran over, and picked him up. She ran down the street carrying Tommy's brother in her arms like a baby, calling for a doctor. The girlfriend ran beside the mother, her hands cupped under her boyfriend's head, trying to catch the blood. Tommy and I were left in the yard. We didn't say anything. We were looking at the rake: the tines sticking up, a trickle of red blood running onto some yellow leaves. All I could think about at that moment was how beautiful it was.

Is this story true? Of course it is — up to a point. As folklorist

Sandra Dolby Stahl says, "For the personal narrative genre to function properly in any storytelling situation, both the teller and the listener must understand that the story—no matter how rhetorically enhanced—is to be accepted as true." So where does the truth of this story come from?

Though it is based on an actual incident from my childhood, I would call it "rhetorically enhanced." The actual event was less dramatic than the one presented in the story and certainly not fatal. Many of the actual facts—the name of the brother, the actions of the mother before she picked up her son—have been removed. In their place, I have substituted a spare plot with a short emotional arc that mimics the action of the rake and turns a pleasant childhood reminiscence into a horror story.

I begin the process by misdirecting the audience to expect a particular kind of story when I say, "It was one of those golden October days." It is easy for the audience to accept this as a factual statement as it usually reminds them of some pleasant experience they have had. This sets the emotional tone and invites them into the world of the story. The invitation is reinforced by an appeal to the senses: "The air was full of the smell of leaves burning."

Then comes a narrative section that grounds us in the mundane, building a case for the everyday and ordinary. "Tommy's older brother was slowly raking leaves into big piles" is followed by the description of kids playing. Now that the audience is committed, I use the introduction of the girlfriend to shift the tone and give the audience a specific image that flirts with a cliché. I want to create the innocence of a remembered past and contrast it with what will follow, so pink has the right emotional weight. A blue or green sweater would not convey the same innocence.

Having introduced the main characters and the situation, I go to the core of the story with a little transitional description: "He forgot about raking, forgot about us." Like a folktale, each image takes us to the next. To increase the tension, I provide a poetic image for the audience: "balancing the handle on his chin, the tines reaching for the sky like he was going to rake clouds."

In performance, the telling of the story slows here and becomes quieter, as if I were sharing a secret. To strengthen the emotional arc I am creating, I describe an experience many people have had—

time slowing down—a sensation associated with uneasiness and accidents. Connecting this sensation with something they have experienced or heard in another tale, the audience members can then feel the remainder of the story, no matter how improbable, as true.

Now the most horrific image in the story comes into play. To really help create a sense of horror, I speed up the telling as I describe the climactic action. The real horror occurs not when the rake strikes the brother, but when the audience accepts this terrible fact without resistance and feels it internally. In the telling, the rake striking the brother is followed by a brief and very intentional silence to let the audience members resolve their own emotional reaction to the image before the story line returns at an accelerated pace.

There is no need to drag the story out because the longer it lasts, the easier it is for the audience to bring logic or critical judgment to bear. I finish off the story with two images: one of action and one of stillness, both involving blood. "The girlfriend ran beside the mother . . . trying to catch the blood" is the first, and "a trickle of red blood ran onto some yellow leaves" is the other. I have made a conscious decision to end with this image.

For many people, the final sentence is the hook that catches them: "All I could think about at that moment was how beautiful it was." It is a very quiet, almost peaceful acknowledgement of my reaction to the event, but—for audience members—potentially the most disturbing. It is a moment that is both a plausible explanation as to why I am telling this story forty years later and the invitation for those hearing the story to re-enter the story to examine their own feelings about what horror is and their response to it.

It is important to remember that the story was not born with this construction. To arrive at this plot, the story was repeatedly told and shaped, with some material added and a lot more pared away until the emotional arc I was looking for was consistently manifest in the audiences' responses. Every descriptive detail in the story was tested, as was the plot and emotional arc, to serve a single purpose: to draw the audience into the dark heart of the story. One of the best ways to find what is right for a story is to tell the same source material in a variety of genres—as tall tales, ghost stories, folk tales, prose poems, oral history, etc.—to see what level of descriptive detail is appropriate to the plot form and emotional arc you are crafting. As an example, the tall tale will allow as much expansive, even exaggerated, detailing as the teller dares insert within the form's humorous, open-ended framework. Meanwhile, poems or ballads require shaping based on patterns of meter and rhyme. Don't be afraid to test many different approaches to stories and to fail. Knowing what doesn't work helps pinpoint what does.

Exercises

1. Select a story you know well. In this example, let's use *Little Red Riding Hood*. On a sheet of paper, draw a horizontal line. At one end of the line mark the first action of the story: Mother tells the girl she needs to go to Grandma's house with the basket of goodies. Now mark the second action: the girl takes the forest path. Mark the third, fourth, and subsequent actions until you've come to the end of the story. This is the narrative line that identifies what happens.

Decide what the narrator of the story feels about those actions. Positive, negative, neutral? Are there points in the story where the narrator expresses or could express anxiety, fear, excitement, or humor? At those points, write what the emotion is or could be. This is the narrator's arc.

Looking at the sequence of actions once again, decide what the major characters in the story feel as they go from one part of the story to the next. How does the girl feel about going to Grandma's house? Is she curious or afraid when she meets the Wolf? How does she feel when she sees "Grandma" in bed? This is the character's arc. You can do one for each major character—one for the girl, one for grandma, one for the wolf—and compare their feelings as the story unfolds.

Finally, think about how the audience hearing or reading this story feels about the action. Are we sympathetic to the girl? Do we approve of her actions and want her to succeed, or do we think she deserves what happens? At what parts of the story do we feel uneasy or fearful? This is the audience's arc. As adults, our emotional involvement in *Little Red Riding Hood* may be minimal, but when we first heard it as children, we were very engaged.

Pick a character in the story. Write or tell the story in such a way as to emphasize that character's point of view. What language would you use to make the wolf the hero instead of the villain? What would you say if you wanted to emphasize the girl's increasing awareness and fear that something is wrong with grandma? Try writing or telling that story now.

Write or tell the story in such a way as to build the emotional response in the audience. What descriptive language would you use to frighten the listener or reader? What if you wanted to make it funny? Where do you put the jokes? Try it now.

2.   Create a story in which the emotion builds to a climax. This might be a ghost story or a joke. Once you have done that, create a second version of the story that is emotionally flat, where there is no build or no climax. What language do you need to use to make the emotional climax satisfying?

3.   Create a story in which the narrator is unreliable either because he or she does not understand what is happening or is lying about what happened. What language do you need to use to let the audience know that the narrator is unreliable? What language would you use to try to make the audience either feel sorry or feel contempt for the narrator?

There will be additional opportunities to craft the emotional arc of a story as we go through the various plot forms. What is critical to remember is that you will have to make decisions about the emotional arcs of the story as well as the narrative actions, and that in the best stories, each set of decisions reinforces the whole of the story.

CHAPTER FOUR

THE PLOT FORMS

"Sameness is the mother of our disgust, variety the surest cure."
Petrarch

Think of the plot as the bones of a story, and the emotional arc as the heart. They should work in unity to create a singular thing of beauty—a story that, when told or read, is forcefully present and inviting. When audience members hear or read such a story, they enter its internal logic and geography willingly, and find that it satisfies, sustains, and remains with them.

There are times when the hero's journey, as universal and potent as it is, feels inadequate to the story we want to tell. There are times when, even if we want to use the familiar journey formula, we need another, less straightforward approach. This is especially true when we want to create original stories that draw their truth and emotional power from philosophical or psychological meanings.

This book examines nine plot forms that I have found work well for the creation of original stories, whether you are crafting a hero's journey or a less traditional piece. They may be arranged as "points on a compass," serving as the guide for the path of story development. The four cardinal points (North, South, East, and West) represent the narrative forms most often used, and the other points represent combinations or interesting variations on the more commonly used forms.

Straight Narrative

Meta-framed   **Digression**

Parallel   **List**   **Revelation**

Regression   **Reversal**

Circular

Each narrative form has particular characteristics, advantages, and limitations. Each is capable of creating a lively, inviting, and fully realized story. Proceeding clockwise around the compass, I will examine each narrative form in detail and include two stories as examples of each form. One example will be a retelling of a traditional fairy tale, *Jack and the Beanstalk*, so that you can see the variations of plot using a single source. The other will be an original story from my repertoire.

I also will include a formula for each plot form that reduces the plot elements to their bare essentials. The formula for the straight narrative, as an example, is expressed as (A-B-C-D-E), meaning that A, the beginning, leads to B, which leads to C, which leads to D, which leads to E, the end. Following that is an identification of the focus of the plot form as a time progression, a point of view or something else. Finally, with each plot form, I will offer book and movie examples that you might have read or seen, or would find valuable to read or see.

CHAPTER FIVE

TRADITION OR HABIT?

"If the plot is to be elegant, then for the ensuing action no important information in the exposition should be irrelevant to the action that ensues."
John Gardner

The Straight-Narrative Plot

Formula: A-B-C-D-End
Focus: Time progression
Book or movie: *Beowulf*
                The Wizard of Oz

It begins at the beginning and moves surely towards the end. As Ruth Sawyer puts it in her classic book *The Way of the Storyteller*, "the development of the folk tale is direct and usually in sequence: because of this, this happened—a series of natural consequences which the mind follows with little effort. The development is cumulative—it builds up to the climax. What explanation follows the climax is usually as brief as the introduction. It may be summed up in a single paragraph. What happens must be inevitable—it must follow a kind of divine logic, be acceptable to all. It must leave the listeners with a complete sense of satisfaction."

While Sawyer is describing the classic folk tale, she might as well be describing the straight-narrative plot form. Each element of the story leads directly to the next, building an unbroken and usually quite economical chain of images and actions.

Let's use an X-ray of a story—an image-by-image model of a familiar tale, *Jack and the Beanstalk*—to see how the form is developed:

> *The cupboard is bare. There is nothing to eat. Mother sends Jack to the market to sell the last thing they have of any value: the cow. On the way, Jack meets a man who offers to trade the cow for some magic beans. With a promise of plenty in hand, he goes home. Jack shows the*

beans to Mother, who is both angry and disappointed that the boy would trade the cow for something as worthless as this. She throws the beans out the window and sends Jack to bed hungry.

With the first light of morning, Jack sees that the beans have grown. He climbs out the window, up the beanstalk, and comes upon a wondrous land. Before him stands a giant house. Still hungry, he goes to the door to ask for something to eat. The Giant's wife takes pity on Jack, feeds him, and then hides him in the pantry when her husband returns. His suspicion aroused that something is amiss, the Giant calls out, "Fe, fi, fo, fum! I smell the blood of a young one! Be he alive or be he dead, I'll grind his bones to make my bread."

The wife placates him with food and wine, and while the Giant sleeps, Jack makes his escape, stealing a bag of gold as he leaves.

He is not content with the gold but returns to the Giant's house, and on successive visits takes the goose that lays the golden eggs and the singing harp. The third time, however, the cry of the harp wakes the Giant, who gives chase. Jack quickly descends the beanstalk and cuts it down. The Giant falls to his death. Jack and his mother live happily ever after.

The function of the straight- narrative plot form is that A does lead to B, and B leads to C. The implied logic of each action supports what comes next, even if it is premised on a suspension of belief to allow for magic beans or a Giant's castle in a land above the earth.

Here, a bare cupboard initiates the action of the story. A cow is traded for beans. A beanstalk grows, and Jack climbs. He meets the Giant's wife. The risk of discovery is followed by successive thefts of gold, the goose, and the harp. There is a climactic chase and a triumphant cutting of the beanstalk. The story ends with the formulaic "happily ever after."

In many traditional narratives, there is only as much description in the text as is needed to convey the action but ample room for the teller to add description to flesh the story out. Think of the folk or fairy tale as a hologram in which a complex whole is compacted into a small space. As you shine the light of performance through the holographic images, they expand and can fill the room.

In other traditional narratives, especially the novel, the basic plot progression is loaded with extra material, from detailed descriptions and the background of characters to musings on matters cultural, historical, or philosophical. Think of Charles Dickens being paid a penny a word for the serial version of *A Tale of Two Cities*, and you can see why he might have had reason to load a simple plot with a wealth of extras. Strip away the textures, however, and what remains is a straight narrative of two men and what they do in the face of a crisis.

Like most tellers, I have stories that come from my childhood. This one uses a straight-narrative form but does not follow the previously discussed journey-of-the-hero formula.

The Knife

When I was a child living in Hibbing, my family would go to my grandmother's farm on weekends. It was a small dairy farm a few miles outside town, with a solid square house set on a little rise, a red barn down the slope next to a pond, and, scattered in between, an outhouse, a garage, the chicken coop, and a sauna. Beyond the outhouse was a small grove of crabapple trees and next to it a fence with 40 acres of rocky soil mostly reserved for hay. My father would help milk the cows or butcher chickens. Being Finns, we would take saunas. Afterwards, my parents would eat fresh baked rolls with their coffee in my grandmother's kitchen.

Mostly I remember the warmth of the kitchen and the smells of coffee and cinnamon rolls baking, stews simmering in big black pots, or stacks of thin, dark-edged pancakes hot off the griddle, covered with unsalted butter and maple syrup. The smell of kerosene, the smell of bacon cooking in cast-iron skillets, of anise seed baked in yeasty warm rolls, of fresh milk still warm from the cow are all called to mind. In my memory, there is always Grandmother's smile. She is always sitting at the table, a

face as round as the full moon with a babushka, sipping
coffee from a cup that was sweetened by the sugar cube
she clenched between her teeth. "Boyka," she would say,
holding me on her lap. "Sumalina boyka." This translated
as her pride that I was a "Finnish boy."

This one time, when I was four or maybe just turning
five, my uncle Uno appeared at the door and motioned for
me to follow him. So I left my mother and Grandmother
in the kitchen and followed him into the living room, past
the table with the lace runner and the open Bible, past the
green horsehair couch, and my dead grandfather's chair
that I had never seen anybody sit in. Through the hallway
and up the stairs to the second story, with each corner
of the house occupied by small bedrooms. Up the creaky
stairs leading to the attic, where he lived, with the slanted
walls marking the roof and the brick chimney marking the
center of the room. One electric light hung by the door,
barely illuminating the room despite the best efforts of the
bare bulb. Across from the door was his narrow bed, and
along the walls his clothes hung on nails. The wedding
and funeral suit hung on a hanger on the furthest nail,
the Sunday shirt next to it, and then the progression of
worn overalls and woolen shirts, long underwear and
jackets, in various states of clean to dirty, marching
towards the door and the laundry thereafter.

This too was a world of smells: Sweat, manure, wet
cotton, musty woolen blankets, the single bottle of Old
Spice he reserved for special events sitting on top of his
dresser next to a comb and shaving mirror.

My uncle was a small man. For many years, I
thought of him as a gnomish figure, tousle haired, watery
eyes, and a toothless grin, hunched over. Now I realize
that if I had spent a good portion of my life in a room
where the only place you could stand straight was in
the center, I might be stooped as well. And it was to that
center he went, to the dresser that seemed too big to have
ever fit through the door or come up the narrow stars.

"Open your hand," he said, and held his out, palm

up, to show me how. I did so. He opened the top drawer
of the dresser. He pulled out something and turned to fix
me in a solemn gaze. "Every Finn should carry a knife at
all times," he told me in a hushed whisper as he placed a
small jackknife in my outstretched hand. "Don't tell your
mother!" he said as he closed my fingers around the small
brown handle of the two-bladed knife.

But the admonition — "Don't tell your mother!" —
was unheard. My entire attention was focused on the
knife. I had a knife. I was a Finn boy with a knife — a
two-bladed jackknife. In my eyes, that knife might as well
have been a sword. As I went back down the stairs, I could
not take my eyes off the knife. With every step, my heart
swelled with pride. I had a knife! I was a man!

Without a moment's hesitation, I marched into the
kitchen, thrust out my hand, and declared that I had
a knife. Without a moment's hesitation, my mother
snatched it away. I couldn't believe it; my knife was gone.
Vanished. I burst into tears and turned to run to my
uncle Uno.

"What's done is done," he said with a shrug. "I told
you not to show it to your mother. Come, we will go
outside and feed the chickens."

A few years ago, we were sitting around the table
telling stories, and I told that one. My mother got up and
left the room. I thought I had upset her, but when she
came back in, she said, "Hold out your hand." When I
did, she put a jackknife into my waiting palm. "You're old
enough for this now."

It was the same knife, the small, brown, two-bladed
knife my uncle Uno had given me thirty years earlier.

The farm is gone now. The forty acres sold to our
cousins to expand their dairy operation. The house sold,
and the barn and sheds demolished, to make way for the
new highway. My grandmother is gone now. She worked
the place until she was eighty-seven, then fell and broke
her hip. Died in a rest home soon after. My uncle Uno is
gone now. Shook himself to death with Parkinson's disease

long ago. All gone. All dead and gone, but I still have the knife. When I hold that knife in my hand, when I tell the story, they are with me still.

This story begins, as any folk tale would, at a point in time and continues along a logical, chronological path to a conclusion. There's nothing flashy here, just a basic, bread-and-butter story in which the substance comes from the progression of images. It begins with an initial scene setting of time, place, and the principal characters. The bulk of the story is a sequence of specific actions that builds tension, reveals character, and sets us up for the conclusion. It ends, as most traditional narratives do, simply, with the world that was turned upside down righted once more.

In crafting the common form of the straight narrative, the first thing to decide on is how it is shaped for reading or telling:

- What is the specific progression of what happens?
- How does it build and release its tension?
- Will it be a story told in present or past tense, or some combination of the two?
- Is it to be told in the first- or third-person voice?

All of the fundamental decisions above must be made as well as the more pedestrian considerations of where does the story begin and where does it end. In structuring this story, I wanted to be faithful to Ruth Sawyer's admonition that the action be a series of natural consequences that the mind follows with little effort and that what happens must be inevitable—it must follow a kind of logic, based not simply on what is said but also what is done and implied.

In describing this plot form and each of the successive ones, I will emphasize the same things: Make conscious decisions about what you include or exclude from the story. Who is telling the story, and why are they telling us this story? Have the plot be an appropriate expression of what the story is about and what it means to you. Make conscious decisions about what the emotional arc of the story is. What changes for the characters in the story? For the story's narrator or the audience? Use details that appeal to the senses to invite the audience into the world of the story. Test the material on a variety of audiences. Shape and reshape material until you are satisfied that this is the story you want to tell and that it can be told in the way you want to tell it.

I do this because I know that readers often will skip around, reading this chapter or that as the mood strikes them. Therefore, I want to make sure you have plenty of opportunities in the book to arrive at an "ah-ha" moment where you understand the connection between what I am saying and the work you want to do. Bear with me, and you'll be rewarded.

While the straight-narrative plot lends itself to compactness, the next—the digressive plot—does the opposite.

Exercises

Fables are stories that teach lessons about human values and behavior using animals as the principal characters. Examples include *Aesop's Fables,* George Orwell's *Animal Farm*, and contemporary movies such as *Finding Nemo*. A fable contains an explicitly stated moral that sums up the lesson it teaches. Many storytellers find it an enjoyable form to work with and an imaginative way in which to express the lesson you wish to teach.

One striking characteristic of fables is that while the animals are displaying human-like behavior and attitudes, there is a high degree of willingness on the part of readers and listeners to learn and retain the lesson because the behaviors and attitudes are ones we recognize.

The power of the fable stems in part from its simplicity, and it is a testimony to the ongoing power of these stories that we continue to use clichés and colloquialisms taken from animal behavior to characterize human activity, like saying someone is "a bull in a china shop" or a "sly dog." However, while we might say a lawyer is "as cunning as a fox," would we as readily suggest that a fox is "as cunning as a lawyer?" This suggests that for the creation of fables, some care should be taken to match the behaviors to be displayed with the popularly accepted images and attitudes the culture has toward the animals in question. If you are in a culture that believes that penguins are cute and harmless, a fable that portrays them as senseless killers who travel in packs and devour whatever gets in their way would not be very well received.

Think carefully—what human-like characteristics and behaviors do we ascribe to the animals you want to populate the fable with? As an example, if you choose a monkey and its central characteristic is curiosity, would you want to create a story whose moral is "there's a right tool for every job"? Would it be appropriate for the monkey in the story to use its curiosity to find or create a tool that will enable it to get what it cannot usually have?

When these stories are properly crafted, the morals seem particularly apt, perfectly suited to comment upon the resolution of the tales. The moral generally is a single phrase or idea that sums up the lesson of the story. Here are some examples of morals taken from a variety of cultures that can and have been used with fables:

- A bad worker blames his tools. (Japanese)
- United we stand, divided we fall. (American)
- A throw of the dice will never abolish chance. (French)
- If the fish had not opened his mouth, he would not have been caught. (Unknown origin)
- A bird in the hand is worth two in the bush. (English)
- Never put off until tomorrow what you can do today. (American)
- It is not the last blow of the axe that fells the tree. (African)
- Money is a terrible master but an excellent servant. (Greek)
- Patience is a garment never worn out. (Persian)

Choose a moral from this list or use the fortune from a cookie. Choose an animal that will be your fable's central character. Remember there should be a consistency between the characteristics and actions of the animal you choose and the way in which the moral of the story is presented. Think about Aesop's *The Tortoise and the Hare* as an example. Each animal was chosen to represent specific characteristics: speedy impulse and steady pace. Now create a story in which the action of the story illustrates your chosen moral.

To help you with this, I suggest that you begin with the moral and then go *backwards*, asking yourself, "What would have come before this?" as you develop the plot line. When it is polished and told, the moral will be a fitting conclusion to the action.

CHAPTER SIX

PLEASANT DETOURS

"And there begins a lang digression about the lords o' the creation."
Robert Burns

The Digressive Plot

Formula: (A-B-C-D-End)
               B1   D1
               B2   D2
                    D3
Focus: Point of view
Book or movie: Herman Melville's *Moby-Dick*
                  Federico Fellini's *Amarcord* or any
                  Marx Brothers' film

The concept of the "road not taken" doesn't apply here. In the digressive plot, there are many detours between the beginning and the end, each adding to the richness of the journey by providing sub-plots, characterizations, or details. The key to successfully telling this kind of story is to not lose the audience's or your train of thought as you work through each digression.

A successful digression begins with a sense of trust between the author and the audience and builds its inevitable excesses piece by piece. For those of you who are familiar with storyteller Bil Lepp's tales, you know that his layering on of improbabilities and absurdities begins almost casually but culminates in something that would be rejected out of hand if he began with it. Even though digressions seem to lead us away from the main plot line, each one should contribute to the audience's understanding or appreciation of the story as a whole.

How far off the beaten path can you go? As far as you need to go to make the story work. For many people, this is a basic and unconscious mode of storytelling. I was once on a trip through Indiana with a friend whose everyday conversational digressions are legendary and frequent. One morning, I decided to not interrupt him and to let him tell one of his stories with as many detours as he was inclined to take. The story began as we were driving past a local beauty shop in Greencastle with him saying that he had gotten a haircut there once. It ended two and a half hours later when we pulled into the parking lot of the student union of the university in Bloomington, with an explanation of why that beauty shop had a red door. Because I was his friend, I found it amusing and perversely entertaining. However, for audience members not trapped in a car, getting them to listen to a long, digressive tale will require a modicum of style, a command of language, and the discipline of very careful structuring.

Here's our reference example, *Jack and the Beanstalk*, with digressions:

> There is nothing to eat so Ma sends Jack to sell the cow. Now Jack loves that cow. So much so that he's taught the cow tricks—how to fetch a stick, how to dance on its hind legs, and more. This is one talented cow—an udder delight, if you please. Why that cow even saved Jack's life once. Seems that the house caught on fire. A spark from the chimney set the thatch ablaze. Well, Jack and Ma were fast asleep, but the cow wasn't. No, sir, that cow broke out of the barn, barged through the door, and moo'ed a wake-up call that sent Jack six inches straight into the air. Once Jack got that cow chased out of the house, he realized that putting out the fire was more important. Well, that cow had already thought of it, and filled a bucket with milk, ready for Jack to throw on the flames. So Jack figures that he owes the cow something. Maybe he can sell the cow and still keep her by having the cow roll over and play dead. The trick doesn't work though, so Jack has to go home with a handful of beans and without a cow. He's so upset, he tosses the beans out the window.
>
> When morning comes, there's a leafy green rope stretching into the clouds, and he climbs the beanstalk all the way up to the Giant's house. Jack knew it was a Giant's house 'cause the door was gigantic. Ten feet. No, taller—twelve feet. No, so tall that a man standing on the

shoulders of another man riding a horse would just be able to feel for the key tucked away on top of the door frame. So Jack, he knocks on the door to see what will happen and when it opens, there's one big woman standing there. She don't see Jack. She calls out for her husband to come home for lunch, and since she said, "Come and get it," Jack scoots on in to see what there is to get. Pretty soon this great big fellow comes through the door. Well, maybe he wasn't as big as Jack expected because he was littler than the Mrs. but he was still twice Jack's size, and Jack was tall for his age. Everyone said that—"Jack, you're a regular beanpole"—which was ironic since it was a case of the pole climbing the vine, not the other way around. Right away, the fellow commences to complaining that he got no respect from other Giants, and he's using language that would've gotten Jack a mouthful of lye soap if he said it. He only stops when he's done ate just about everything on his plate and settled into a big chair to take a nap.

Jack figures it is time to light out when the Mrs. goes to take the garbage out. He's headed for the door when he sees a bag just full of gold coins sitting beside the big snoozer. Well, a man's got to have something to show for his trouble because no one is going to believe him if he says he was visiting a Giant's house unless he done got some proof. So he grabs the bag. Whooo, it's heavy. Like carrying-rocks-uphill or the-last-hay-bale-of-the-afternoon-into-the-loft heavy. Now Jack, he knows something about heavy. There was a time in his life when he wanted to be a champion weightlifter. Every day he'd go out to the barn and lift the heaviest thing he could grab a hold of. Started with chickens. There wasn't much to it, so he'd moved on to grabbing pigs back in the day when they had pigs and later the cow. Might have been the reason it stopped giving milk when it saw Jack coming in the door. Jack just squares up his shoulders and bends to it. He's going to bring that sack back if it kills him. And as he starts down the beanstalk, he thinks the weight of that sack is making him slide so as to wear away the sides of his pants. The leaves are getting all busted up, and Jack's skidding along after the bag o' gold, which is just about falling if it weren't for the resistance Jack is providing at the cost of his britches. They was almost new pants. Had just been worn by one or two other fellows before they was handed on down to him.

Well, it hadn't been a day or two before Jack thinks to himself that there ought to be more where that gold came from. The beanstalk was still there and once he climbed it, the Giant's house was right where he left it as well. It wasn't any harder to get in the second time than it was the first. In fact, things pretty much repeated themselves exactly as they had before, as if it was one of those dreams you sometimes have where you done something you done before. Yup, it was all the same except for the part about the gold coins. Weren't any coins to be seen. But then old Jack sees the most amazing thing. A goose sits right down on the floor and pops a golden egg out when that Giant fellow says, "Lay!" Jack knows what's got to be done, and he grabbed the goose and headed for the door. Trouble was the goose was almost as big as he was, and though it didn't weigh near as much as the gold coins, that bird was almost as stubborn as Jack was when it came to doing his lessons. Didn't want to, and Jack didn't actually carry the goose so much as wrestle it to the door. Then he couldn't figure out how to get the door open, so he plucks a feather and the goose lets out a squawk and the Mrs.—she says, "QUIET goosie! You'll wake the Mr." Sure enough, she opens the door and lets the goose scoot out, and Jack just circles around her backside to follow the goose out without her seeing him.

Well, I'll tell you getting that goose down the bean stalk wasn't much easier than getting the sack of gold down, but he held on to the stalk with one hand and the goose with the other, and they made out. And that should have been enough for Jack, but not a week goes by before he's thinking about what else might be found in that awfully big house. Maybe a flying carpet like he had heard

about in stories. That would make getting home a lot
easier then shimmying up and down the vine. Jack could
just imagine himself sitting right square in the middle of
a rug and saying, "Rise up!" and then holding on when
it commences to shiver and shake and leave the ground.
How would you steer the thing? Maybe he'd just grab one
corner or another and lift to make it turn. Pull back the
edge like it was the reins of a horse and yell, "Whoa"" to
make it stop. Now a carpet like that would make it worth
the trouble to climb all the way back to the clouds. So off
he went.

This time, it was a harp that sung by itself. At first,
Jack didn't think it was worth as much as a bag of gold or
a goose that lays golden eggs, but the harp sure did know
how to sing. She—and Jack figured anything singing
so sweet must be a she—sang about as pretty as any
songbird he ever heard. She knew all kinds of songs—
long, sad songs that made you want to cry, and songs
so funny he had to bite his tongue to keep from laughing
out loud, and songs that had no name but made you feel
like you was in the bestest place in the whole world. Jack
knew what he had to do, and he wanted to do it more than
anything.

Here's the trouble for you. Just because Jack wanted
the harp for his own did not mean that harp wanted to be
had. Soon as he picked her up, she commences to shouting,
"Stop thief!!!" The Giant stopped mid-snore and opened
one eye. "Help," the harp cries, "I am being taken from
you." Jack could see the Giant trying to understand what
was going on and put his hand over the harp's mouth
to make her shut up, but she bit him and went back to
hollering at the Giant. Then, like another kind of dream,
a really bad one where you also know what's going to
happen next isn't right or pretty, the Giant is standing
and roaring out curses so foul the paint is peeling off the
wall. Jack is standing at the door trying to figure out how
to get it open when the Giant dives for the harp. Jack sees
him coming and steps aside, and the Giant crashes into

the door, busting it up something fierce. Jack throws the harp out a crack and throws himself out after her.

He never ran so fast in his life. He never worried less about the rip of pants or the burn of flesh as he slid down the vine. He could hear the clamor and bellow, and it was as good a way to judge distance as the sound of the hunting dogs in the woods. All the time, that damned harp is wailing so as to make him deaf in one ear, and he's telling it to shut up but it pays him no mind. At the bottom of the beanstalk, he puts her down and runs over to the woodpile to get the axe.

Nothing like a good axe, or maybe, nothing like a good sharp blade on an axe. A good axe goes through a piece of cordwood like a knife through butter. It's all in the motion. You move with the axe, accelerating as you come down, square on the top, and let the weight of it follow the grain. You use an axe on a tree, and you begin with a downward stroke, not too deep, and then an upward stroke to notch away a piece of the tree the width of the blade. Over and under, left and right. With every stroke more of the tree is removed until the weight of what is left begins to press down, straining the wood and binding the blade. That's when you go to the other side and begin again. Eventually, the tension is released, and the tree falls toward the first cut.

Jack didn't have time for niceties now. There was no strategy for cutting the beanstalk. It was just swing and swing again. The first blow made the whole thing shake like he had plucked a guitar sting. "Swing," Jack says to himself and swing he did. When it snaps, jump away. Oh, there was a terrible crash when the Giant hit the ground some mile or two away, but Jack didn't hear it. He had picked up the harp, gone in the house, bolted the door, and told Ma that he was really, truly done adventuring. Then he sat himself in a big old chair and asked the harp to sing something comforting. For the first time, the harp did what he asked.

Digressive plots provide an ideal base for building a humorous story. Each digression allows the teller to develop observations, jokes, and asides that create an overall sense of "funny" for the story, even if the central plot line is not particularly humorous. As an example of that, one of my favorite digressive stories from my repertoire illuminates an unfortunate accident with digressions about smoking and the nature of guilt:

Smoking

When I was in junior high, my family was living just outside Buffalo, New York, in a little town called Hamburg. We lived on a cul-de-sac sandwiched between some farms and a forest that went halfway to Pennsylvania.

The Tracys lived next door. They were a big family with many girls and two boys: Sonny and his brother Quickie. They went to the same school as we did, rode the same bus, and were in the same Boy Scout troop, before we were forced to resign in disgrace, that is. Those two plus my brother and myself were your basic pre-teen trouble magnets if ever there were any.

I don't know why he was called Quickie. No one ever said. Maybe it was because he was both sneaky and fast. I knew that was true because one of Quickie's principal jobs was to steal cigarettes from Mrs. Tracy. That wasn't so tough though, because Mrs. Tracy—hell, like the whole family—was a nudist. Yes, it was a real shock for my mother the first time she went over to their house to borrow a cup of sugar when Mrs. Tracy came to the door wearing an apron and a smile. Walked around the house naked and was a chain smoker. Can you see where I'm going? The fact she had no pockets was the source of my introduction to old Devil Nicotine. She kept a pack of cigarettes in every room. Very convenient for when she wanted to light up. Very convenient for Quickie, because all he had to do was go from room to room taking just one cigarette from each pack to get us an afternoon of real smoking fun.

Now this one afternoon, we were sitting up in the hayloft of George Wheeler's barn. George was the other

*member of our gang. Same school, same bus, same Boy
Scout troop. We were lounging around the hay bales,
practicing to be men—working on our smoking technique.
You know, how to hold the cigarette so the snipers won't
see the light and shoot you. How to let the butt dangle
at just the right angle from your lip like James Dean or
Bogey did so the smoke swirls up in front of your face,
leaving you in a cloud of mystery. Sonny was having a
lot of trouble with that one. He'd dangle a cigarette at a
jaunty angle, and the smoke would just curl right up his
nose, producing some of the most spectacular coughing
and wheezing I had ever seen. So there we are practicing
to be men— smoking, holding the cigarette real stylish,
and telling lies about girls. Bragging about kissing Shelia
Dempsey. Everyone but Quickie said they had. He was too
young to appreciate her B-cup charms. I knew I was lying.
She wouldn't give me the time of day, so I figured they all
were lying too.*

*There was one thing that was absolutely true about
Shelia Dempsey. She was real pretty but, oh boy, she was
one tough girl. Used to hang out with the Lackawanna
steel mill kids. Rolled her skirts up. The other girls thought
she was a tramp but most of them were just jealous of the
attention the boys paid her. Every eighth-grade guy I knew
had a hard-on for her, and she would play one against the
other for fun. She French kissed Mike Stevens in the hall
after lunch. I knew that because I saw her walk into the
girl's bathroom with a big smile and him wiping lipstick
off his mouth before he went into the classroom. Oh, how I
wanted to have that problem.*

*It was at that very moment that George said, "Watch
this." Then, with a gesture that was as economical as it
was beautiful, he flicked the cigarette away, the thumb and
middle finger plucking the Benson & Hedges 100 from his
thin lips, the index finger snapping forward, extending to
point at the path of the departing cigarette. The cigarette
began with a slow tumble and then, righting itself, flew
with the filter tip first and the burning ash behind, the tip*

a fiery red as the cigarette arched into the darkness of the barn. Watching the thin trail of smoke that followed the curve of the white cylinder through sunlight and shadow, I was reminded of the cheesy rockets in sci-fi movies—really fake and yet beautiful to look at.

Before you could say, "Geeez, that was a dumb thing to do," the cigarette landed amid the loose hay and set it on fire. We just stared wide-eyed as the flames shot up and the smoke filled the hayloft. Did we put out the fire? No, we panicked, threw ourselves out of the hayloft, and ran for the bushes.

About the time the flames were coming out the barn doors and the smoke looked like someone was having a very big cookout, we got tired of lying in the dirt panting like dogs that have been chasing cars. We could hear the fire engines coming up the road. We saw them roar into the yard with Dr. Herges, our family dentist and chief of the Volunteer Fire Department, hanging on the door of the pump truck, leading the charge. My brother said, "You know, if we weren't guilty, we'd be standing right there watching the whole thing up close instead of hiding in these bushes."

"You're right," Sonny shouts, and he gets up to go to watch the flames and water and firemen up close and personal.

We were watching the firemen pumping water into the hayloft when the Shadow of Doom, George Wheeler's father, fell over us. I didn't even have to look up—all I had to see from the corner of my eye was this immense hand put the vice grip on George's shoulder. Man, his hands were big, baseball-glove big. And when he clamped his fingers on George, I swear I could hear bones break. But it was his other hand that really worried me, because that was the one that went sliding into George's pocket, fished around a little, and extracted a single cigarette like some graceful bird plucking some pale worm off the rain-washed sidewalk.

"Is this yours, George?"

George didn't say anything. He grimaces like he just ate something sour and has to pretend it isn't, and points to Sonny. Sonny points to me. I point to my brother. My brother points to Quickie. Quickie, with nowhere else to go, points back to George. With the circle of guilt fully traversed, Mr. Wheeler turned to us with one of those I'm-going-to enjoy-this looks parents get when they know they've caught you in the worst possible foolishness and are going to make you squirm before they give you the whack you know is coming. We just stared at the ground or the fire hoses or something. Then he said, "Boys, I think you've had enough smoke for the day. You ought to go home now and wait for me to call your parents."

Call my parents? We ran home rehearsing a dozen different explanations for how the barn accidentally caught on fire. It was lightning. No good—there wasn't a cloud in the sky. A cow kicked over a lantern. Where had I heard that one before? No, Mr. Wheeler had electric lights. A cow kicked over an electric light? Not likely. OK, what about spontaneous combustion? Yeah, that happens. A big pile of cow pies just got so hot they stopped baking and exploded into flames. By the time we got home, I had almost talked myself into blurting out the truth. "Geezzz, Ma, we were just smoking, and set the barn on fire."

An hour went by, and nothing happened. Six. Twelve. Every time the phone rang, my heart raced, and I broke into a sweat. I would hear the ring start and before it could finish, I would jump to answer it, figuring that if it was Mr. Wheeler, I could pretend to be my dad. It was always somebody else. A day went by, and the call still hadn't come. I was so nervous I wanted to drink a big cup of coffee to calm me down. That night, I lay in bed praying to God that it would come so my Dad would kill me and get it over with. I prayed that it wouldn't come and offered God all kinds of desperate bargains in exchange—that I'd work very hard in school, that I wouldn't tease my little sisters, or, if God would spare me this terrible trouble, I would do whatever He wanted me to do. I'd even become a nun. I was so desperate for divine intervention that I even offered to quit smoking, but reneged on that promise while walking home from the bus the very next day.

That's one of the things about being in trouble. When it comes sure and swift, you can take it and get on with your meteoric rise to juvenile delinquency or sorrow, or whatever it is that those adult authority figures who caught you are suggesting is your future path. Like the time I was caught with the satirical version of a PTA notice I had written. Old Sister Emma, she didn't waste any time. She bore down on us sitting and laughing in the back of the classroom like a torpedo in those old submarine movies—silent, deadly, unseen—exploding in black and white beside Jane Muntz to snatch the note with one hand and my ear with the other. She marched the two of us up to the front of the room while telling me, and everyone else, that idle hands were the Devil's workshop, but idle minds were worse, much worse. She made me read the note, asking what I thought was funny about the PTA. Everything? Whack! Nothing? Whack! Another swift blow of her yellow yardstick, and she sent me back to my seat to contemplate the fact that I was no James Thurber, which was pretty good since the only thing I knew about Thurber, for sure, was that he was dead. But that trouble happened and was over. I had taken the blows, and I could hold my head high on the playground, knowing that I'd been caught by the best of them and got off pretty easy.

But the trouble that's waiting to happen is another thing entirely. It's awful, knowing that there's going to be punishment and pain but not knowing when. The terrible waiting, day after day, for the black cloud to appear, sure that if you let down your guard and have a good time— wham!—you'll get caught. I was spending a jittery week waiting for my father to find out and then turn three shades of fuming, sputtering, and embarrassed because he didn't find out immediately. I was sure that he'd have me sitting in a chair, looking at me like I was a bug, trying to figure out whether to just squash me and be done with *it, or delay it until after he gave the lecture on owning up to a mistake when it happens. Yeah, like any kid wants to volunteer for punishment. No matter what happened, the punishment wouldn't be as bad as the waiting for it to happen, but wait I did.*

The call never came, or if it did, my parents never said anything about it. Sonny's parents never got a call. And a couple of days later, when I saw George, he whispered that his old man hadn't even spanked him or anything like that, but that he had made George sit on the porch and smoke a whole pack of unfiltered Camels, one right after another. It seemed like a weird thing to do, but George said that he'd sort of lost his interest in smoking for a while.

A little later, I lost mine too. Not because of the barn burning down, or Quickie not being able to get any more cigarettes, or anything like that. I quit smoking because when Mary Ellen Foster kissed me in the back of the bus, she told me that she wouldn't kiss anybody who smoked. But that is another story.

How many digressions were in that story? Let's see: there was one about the Tracys as a family, one about smoking as seen in the movies, one about Shelia Dempsey, and one about trouble with a sub-digression about Sister Emma. So there's at least four. None of them are very long. Given the right situation, each of those points of departure could lead to an extended detour, or be treated as separate stories created around a common theme.

The basic function of the digression is twofold: to provide character or background, and to provide an additional emotional build. As background, it allows the storyteller to add texture to his or her material, to create a worldview, and to share history and cultural references with the audience. As an example, in my story, each of the digressive elements about the Tracys— being nudists, how we got cigarettes—supports the basic thrust of the plot line but also provides a sense of who they are. Likewise, the digression about being in trouble could function as a sympathy device encouraging audience members to identify with the teller's plight and allowing them to think about their own views (or memories) of punishment.

As entertaining as digressions can be, the basic rule of "less is more" is at work here. As I said, every digression should support the whole, moving the story and the audience towards a satisfying conclusion. If the digression doesn't exercise a little restraint in terms of making the whole function, let it go, and get on with the story you want to tell.

Though many digressive stories milk the humorous potential of a tale, you can just as easily work tragic or romantic emotional tangents into the digressive plot form. The digressive story can also be told from any point of view—first, second or third person—and in the present or past tense.

The choice of how many digressions, of what kind, and of what length is the writer's, but you always have to be cognizant of the balance between enough digression to flesh out the material and what the audience will accept. When digressions fail, the story can be an awful mess. Digressions usually fail because they have not been consciously chosen and shaped. This is true of both written and oral stories. In the proper setting, when the audience gives you permission to indulge the digressive impulse, you can make a conscious decision to use digressions based on which ones are available to you, where they lead, and how they will support the telling of the story. If a digression has the potential to be a complete story, you have to be all the more careful about what is included. Otherwise, you will end up with a mess of loosely related tales instead of a unified, single story.

Exercises

1. Pick a topic. Let's use your neighborhood as an example. On a set of three-by-five cards, write down various aspects of what you know about your neighborhood. On one card, you might describe the physical appearance of the place. How big is it? What does it look like? Who lives there? On another card, you might write some facts about the history of the place—as an example, what has changed over the years? On other cards, write descriptions of particular people and their relationships to the place or to each other. You can use as many cards as you want, but limit each card to one particular feature of the neighborhood. These will be the basis for your digressive story.

Pick a character from the neighborhood and, using a second set of cards, map out the progression of what happens to that character. Now, decide how many digressions your story will contain. Look over the various cards you've created, and decide which pieces of information you could put in the story and where. Physically lay out the cards. Place the cards describing what happens in the story in a horizontal line. Place the digressions in vertical lines beneath the points in the narrative where you want to insert them.

Create an outline of a story using the various digressions you've chosen. Since every digression should propel the entire story forward, you should pay attention to the transitions from the main narrative line to your digressions and back to the main story again. Now write or tell that story. Does it work? Is it satisfying? What needs to be added or subtracted to the narrative and/or the digressions to have the story flow smoothly from beginning to end?

2. The placement of digressions can make or break a story. Find a story that has digressions within it, and identify each one. Write the central image or theme of each digression on a card. Place those cards in a hat or box or simply shuffle them randomly, and place them face down. Write out the elements of the main narrative on cards, and arrange the cards in a line. Now pick a card from the set of digressions and place it beneath the second narrative card. Pick another card randomly from the digression cards, and place it beneath the digression card you just put down. Pick a third digression card, and place it below the fourth narrative card. Repeat the pattern until all of the digression cards are face up under a narrative card or another digression card.

Since this selection process is determined by chance, it is probable that the digressions will not fit the spaces they are in. They may seem clunky and oddly ordered. The task is to change the story, adding material as needed to make the digressions work. Feel free to add new characters or digressions to arrive at a satisfactory and complete story.

Once you have written or told the story using the cards as they are arranged, select any two digressions and have them trade places. Now, write or tell another version of the story based on the new arrangement of digressions. Does this improve the story? Why?

Do not be afraid to play. Do not be afraid to fail to have a satisfying story. This is an instance where the practice of arranging and rearranging the elements of the story is more important than the results.

CHAPTER SEVEN

IN PLAIN SIGHT

"The more original a discovery, the more obvious it seems afterwards."
Arthur Koestler

The Revelation Plot

Formula: A-B (implied)-C-D-B (revealed)-End
Focus: Time progression
Book or movie: Raymond Chandler's *The Big Sleep*
              The Sixth Sense

Here is the plot form we usually associate with the classic "who done it?" of detective stories or the "gotcha" endings of *The Twilight Zone*, where the story leads to and depends on the discovery of the missing elements of the tale. It appears to be a straight narrative but within the progression of events, some critical fact is withheld from the audience until the end. Or, there are narrative elements that focus your attention away from the critical pieces until they are needed to solve the puzzle.

The best versions of this are the stories that let you see that what is finally revealed was there all along. Think about *The Sixth Sense* and how the revelation is handled. When you come to the end of the movie and realize what the actual situation is, you can go back and see how the clues are presented in the story but downplayed until the end.

The common wisdom regarding classic detective fiction holds that all the elements of the answer *must* be present in the story. You can misdirect or toss in red herrings, but it is considered bad form to pull a metaphorical rabbit out of the hat in a flourish if you didn't have the hat on stage from the beginning. The construction of a good revelation plot is harder than it looks. The key is to provide enough information for audience members to see what they missed when you're done, but not so much that they arrive at the solution before you're ready to reveal it, or, worse, that they're disappointed when the last piece of the puzzle is in place.

There are many good examples of this kind of revelation plot, ranging from Agatha Christie to the classic TV series *Columbo* to the many versions of *CSI*, so I will not say a lot about the mechanics of structuring it. I would encourage you to read or view many examples of this form and literally chart out for yourself the elements of the stories. What is presented and in what order? What is withheld or implied? What is revealed and how? Does it satisfy your logical and emotional needs for a resolution?

Here's one of my stories, a revelation narrative as a ghost story for our times:

David

Whether it was the driver of the car or the gasoline truck who fell asleep at the wheel is unknown. The result was the same. They met on the two-lane, blacktop road. When they did, the corn standing in the Illinois farm field was scorched by the heat of the blast.

That same evening, Bill McCarthy and I were drinking in a black hole of a bar called the Four Queens. We were doing what we had done for the previous forty days and nights. Accepting what God provided, or at least what Bill's girlfriend, Trish the waitress, provided. Mistakes and other people's rejected orders. Black Russians with not enough Russian. Screwdrivers with stripped treads and Manhattans that had too much Brooklyn to taste right. We were too poor and too thirsty to care, so we drank what arrived at the table. By the end of the evening, as with the ones that had preceded it, we needed some mutual help holding each other up to negotiate the path home.

Trish and Bill deposited me at my door and stumbled off towards their apartment above the plumbing store. After fumbling for the key, I resolved to leave the door unlocked the next time. The stairs seemed like a very long climb, and I'm sure I stopped once or twice on the way up. Sometimes you just don't want to take off your clothes. You know that if you bend over to take off your shoes, you will fall and not get up. So I didn't take them off. I just lay on the bed, listening to the too-loud crickets, and watched the room slowly spin its way to oblivion.

Maybe it was a dream. "The hours—gone. The days, weeks—gone. The years—all gone. How much time is left for you?" I opened my eyes and saw a shape of a man standing at the foot of the bed. Who was this? How did he get here?

"Get up," he whispered and moved down the hall to the bathroom. I followed on unsteady feet.

I stood in the dark bathroom, my head pressed against the mirror. I was told once that when you look in the mirror in a dark room, you could see angels or demons. I didn't know if this apparition was either of those but I heard the now-familiar voice say it again: "The hours gone. The days, weeks—gone. The years—all gone. How much time is left for you?" I thought I recognized that voice.

"David," I asked. "Is that you? Aren't you supposed to be in St. Louis?" I turned to see if he was there.

The shadow seemed to reach out, touch a finger to my lips, like you do when marking a secret. "Sssshhh!" The touch was cold, my mouth going numb as I stood there listening to the soft refrain by my ear like the fluttering of a curtain lifted by the night wind. "The hours—gone. The days, weeks—gone. Mine are done. How much is left for you?"

I felt a wave of sadness fill me. How long I stood there weeping before I went back to bed and a troubled sleep, I could not tell you. This much I know: sometime in the morning, the phone rang. When I answered it, a voice that seemed to come from a great distance said that my friend, David Daarst—a member of Christian Brothers, a Catholic religious order, who had burned draft files with the Berrigans and other pacifists in Catonsville, Maryland, to protest the Vietnamese War—had been killed in a head-on collision while driving across Illinois the night before.

When I heard the news, I remembered something

that had once made David laugh. It was a scene in one
of Carlos Castenada's Don Juan books where Carlos and
Don Juan are driving across the desert at night. Carlos
looks in the mirror and sees lights appear and begin to
overtake them. For no reason he can explain, he gets
nervous and remarks on it to Don Juan. The shaman
calmly says that the headlights are Death coming for
them. Now Carlos gets panicky and looks in the mirror
again. The lights are gone, and with their disappearance,
he feels a wave of relief. Don Juan laughs. "Sometimes",
he says, "Death likes to drive with the lights turned off."

Like many good ghost stories, there is a deliberate
sparseness to this one. At the start, I establish the event that must
be known to complete the story, though what is withheld is the
meaning of that image. Then, I shift gears to establish what I hope is
a scene the audience may have experienced or witnessed, building
the framework for the "truth" of what will come next. The heart of
the story, an inebriated individual seeing an apparition, is presented
as a series of images framed in dislocation and allows the audience
to discount the images as drunken imagination or take them as fact.
Finally, the revelation is a very short section that connects what has
happened to the opening and finishes the tale. It is followed by a
coda, which is as much a comment on the "how much time is left for
you" refrain as it is on the inevitability of death.

The sleight of hand required for a successful revelation does not
need to be big or elaborate. You can craft a large impact from small
adjustments, just as, in the trajectory of a rocket, a change of a few
degrees at lift-off could mean the difference between landing on the
moon and flying into the void.

Let's look at the effect a few words of revelation can have in this
version of *Jack and the Beanstalk*:

Looking out the window, young Jack sees the
beanstalk. If only he could climb those green tendrils,
he could have an adventure. He could get away from
the grinding poverty and misery of his life. The cow he
loved has been sold at the market. His mother weeps.

His miserly stepfather is unrelenting in his cruelty.
There is nothing but backbreaking work and hunger
morning, noon, and night at home. There is nothing in
the cupboard.

He imagines himself going up the beanstalk and
coming to a new place, a grander place, to the land of
Giants. Yes, he'll do it. Suppose he found a Giant's
house, filled to the rafters with all the good things in
life. Suppose a kind woman was there and took pity on
him. She would give him a place to rest. The Giant's wife
would be good to him. She would feed him warm, buttered
bread and jam.

But the Giant husband is evil. He is cruel to his wife
and hates her for her kindness to Jack. The Giant hates
Jack and intends to "grind his bones to bake his bread."
He's mean and greedy and has a lot of money hidden in
the house. No one can find it, but Jack is smart enough to
figure out where it is kept and small enough to reach it.
He will take the gold just to spite the Giant.

Jack steals the Giant husband's money to bring
home as a gift for his own sweet mother. Each time he
does so, he comes closer to having the Giant catch him
taking the gold coins from the purse. Finally, he is caught
with gold in hand, and the Giant's rage makes his blood
run cold, his eyes murderous. Jack must run for his life.
Terror follows hard on his footsteps, the Giant shouting
and raining blows upon young Jack's back. Look, there's
the axe. He hears a voice, shouting, "Use it, JACK!!"
Jack turns to face the Giant, and with a well-placed blow,
brings him crashing down.

With the Giant dead, Jack can finally be happy. He
can have the gold and finally take care of his mother
the way she deserves to be treated. Yes, that's what Jack
thinks, but when she looks at the dead body, there is no
thanks from his mother. "Son," she says, "how could you
do this to your stepfather?"

In this twist on the familiar tale, all the elements of the revelation plot are there, but they are unobtrusive. At the end, you realize that a single word—"imagines" —was what set the deception in motion. When you understand that the "dreaming Jack" of the first part of the story sees his stepfather as the cruel Giant, the pieces fall into place, and the familiar fairy tale takes on a theme of patricide when the mother asks her question.

Jokes as Revelations

Not all revelation plots need to be heavy. Revelation also is the basis for the basic punch-line joke. One of the clearest examples I know comes from August Rubrecht, a professor of English literature at the University of Wisconsin. This is from his workshop on humor:

> *A man and a woman are having a romantic candlelight dinner in a fancy restaurant. Suddenly, the man clutches his napkin and falls under the table. The waiter, seeing this happen, comes over to ask the woman if her husband is all right. She replies, "Unfortunately, he is—he just came through the restaurant door."*

The logic this story sets up is one that leads the waiter (and the audience by proxy) to assume that the woman was having dinner with her husband. When she reveals that the man who has fallen to the floor is not her husband, we laugh, not because she might be unfaithful, but because we have been caught making a false assumption. It is the reversal of logic that makes the story funny. The revelation that changes our thinking is implied in the first line of the joke (it says, "A man and a woman are having dinner," not "a husband and wife") but not made explicit ("he just came through the restaurant door") until the final line of the story.

Revelation narratives usually are told in the first or third person and in either present or past tense. I will offer you a caution about the problem with the first-person voice in a revelation. Because the first-person narrator, especially when speaking in the present tense, is limited to knowing what that character can know at the moment he or she is speaking, it becomes more difficult to set up a revelation. When the narrator "gets it," people in the audience have to do two things at once. First, they have to understand what happened, and, at the same time, they need to be able to be "smarter" than the narrator to understand why the narrator didn't get it before this moment. This is why most first-person revelation narratives are done in the past tense. It is so much easier to explain what happened after the fact.

The next plot form we will look at is another kind of revelation, but with the reversal plot form, what is revealed is not in the story but in the audience's response to the story.

Exercises

1. Decide on a narrative, and arrange it on a series of cards with one central image or action on each card. Lay those cards out in order. Pick what you want to reveal, and take that card out of the sequence. However, it is not enough to simply remove information. You should substitute a transition card for the missing piece of narrative, writing out what information you need to keep or suggest from the card you've removed before moving to the next part of the story. Take the card you've removed, and place it where you want the revelation to happen. Again, though, it is not enough to simply place the card here. You should create two additional cards: one to focus the reader's or the audience's attention on what is going to be revealed (i.e., to set the stage) and another to smooth the transition from the revelation to whatever is the next part of the narrative. You should now have the outline of a basic revelation narrative. Read or tell it to another person. Ask them if it works. If it does, congratulations. If it doesn't, ask that person what he or she needs more or less of for the story to work. Decide on what adjustments you want to make, and share your story with someone who has not read or heard it before.

2. Explore placing the revelation at different points in the story. What difference does it make if it is in the middle or at the end? In a joke, the revelation is usually the punch line, and nothing follows. If you put the revelation in the middle of a joke, is it still a joke or has it become simply a humorous story?

3. Consider what is at stake in revealing the missing information. Is there a value in revealing only one important thing, or in having a small series of revelations that leads up to a large one, as is frequently done in detective stories? Try creating a story in which you reveal only one important fact (as I did in the *Jack and the Beanstalk* example). Now, try creating a story where you reveal a series of small things, each of which gives the reader or audience a better understanding of character, emotion, or actions.

CHAPTER EIGHT

THE MIRROR

"Look in a mirror and one thing's sure; what we see is not who we are."
Richard Bach

The Reversal Plot

Formula: A–B–C–D-C1-B1-A1-End
Focus: Point of view
Book or movie: Kazuo Ishiguro's *The Remains of the Day*

The reversal plot form is a sleight of hand in which various elements of the story are the mirror images of each other. The reversal appears to proceed along a straight-narrative path, but it sets up changing interpretations of the core information. What begins as black ends as white. What was unquestioned is now suspect. The power of the story comes from the careful creation of structured scenes and actions that invite the audience members to make a transition in how they think about the story and the way in which those transitions shift the meaning of the tale. This is a plot form in which the development of the emotional arc, especially the audience's, is critical.

Ishiguro's *The Remains of the Day* is a good example of this plot form. The actions of the main character do not change from the start to finish but our understanding of them does, and what seemed like admirable duty in the beginning seems cowardly in the end.

Since it is a variation of the straight narrative, the reversal often is mistaken as an easy form to structure. However, developing a successful story using these mirroring techniques requires careful attention to the placement and timing of descriptive details and images within the plot progression. People in the audience do not want to like a character and then be given a reason to dislike him or her, only to find later in the story that they are supposed to like the character again. Audiences want a kind of clarity in their stories that is at odds with the shifting judgments of real life. Otherwise, they feel like they are being toyed with.

Language choices are critical in these tales, for they serve as the basic tool to shape the audience's understanding and emotional responses. You have to choose both when and how you want to shift the audience's understanding and then set the mechanisms in place to accomplish a seamless transition. A key to doing this is to create four columns: one for the narrative progression, which will mostly list actions; one for the emotional arc of the characters; one for the emotional arc of the audience (what it feels about the central character or the course of action taken at the beginning of the story and what it feels at the end); and one for the emotional arc of the narrator, which will mostly list the language or images the narrator will use to create the mirror effect. This is the master map of the story that will let you see how each of the emotional arcs is manifest as the narrative proceeds. When you see places where the action or images do not fit with the audience emotional arc you want to create, you will know what you need to work on to find the right image or tone to move from the one understanding to its mirror.

Consider a version of *Jack* in which the basic narrative remains the same as we have been telling it but several crucial images are reversed. The opening image is of the cupboard:

> *The cupboard is bare. A single skinny mouse searches in vain for a crumb. Mother sits at the table, her head in her hands, tears running down her cheeks. What are they to do? What are they to do?*

Later in the story, a second crucial image lends itself to contrast:

> *The beanstalk seemed to Jack to be a thick, green rope thrown into the sky, taut and inviting. The leaves, as broad as elephants' ears, wave like green flags in the breeze, as if signaling to Jack that they will support his weight. The broad root gripped the earth, not moving an inch as Jack put his foot upon the first stem and began to climb.*

In telling Jack as a reversal, we could choose any number

of images to shift, but the most important will be an image that
shifts our feelings about Jack or the Giant from one of sympathy
to revulsion or from dislike to empathy. Let's reverse how the
Giant is presented. In the first image, let's play to the conventional
stereotype.

> *Jack looked out from his hiding place to see what the
> Giant might be doing. The first thing he saw was a boot
> so big, it would take the full hide of a cow to make it, and,
> above that, a leg like the trunk of a tree. His eye went up
> and up until it saw the face red and wrinkled, eyes half
> shut with anger, and the terrible mouth open as if he could
> swallow Jack whole. He heard the teeth grind and then
> silence as the Giant stopped, cocked his head, and listened
> for the sound of Jack's wild beating heart.*

Then, near the end of the story, this image will be literally
reversed to give the Giant a softer, more human response to Jack's
theft.

> *Jack could swear that he heard the Giant's heart
> break, the wild beating deafening him as the great
> man stood silent and open-mouthed watching the harp
> disappear down the hall. Jack did not look back but if he
> had, he would have seen the face red and wrinkled, the
> tears streaming down, calling out for his beloved solace,
> his most prized gift of Heaven. Through his tears, the
> Giant resolved to do what he must to regain his happiness
> and lifted one great trembling leg and then another, faster
> and faster until the sound of his boots told Jack exactly
> what the Giant was doing and drowned out the cries of
> the harp.*

That image will be followed by the reversal of the beanstalk
image, creating a sense of apprehension, focused on how
difficult it is to cut the now too-thick vine down:

> *The beanstalk like a steel cable, taut, the green life force*

singing with the vibration of the Giant sliding down like an avenging angel. Jack, knee-deep in the tangle of root, wielding the small axe, saw that it was useless to think a single blow would cut through it. Panic called his name and then the rush of necessity as he swung the axe, again and again, seeming to make no progress. In his panic, he believed the beanstalk would not yield, and if it did not, all would be lost.

To complete the mirroring effect, we will use a final image of peace and plenty that returns to our opening with mother and cupboard:

The cupboard is filled so full the doors cannot be closed. Candy and jams, bread, and sausage line the shelves. Fat mice slide down the sides of flour sacks. Mother sits at the table, laughing so hard at Jack's recounting of the tale, tears run down her cheeks.

The mirroring can be of an image, action, emotion, or psychological condition. The crucial decision is not which elements to mirror but how to give them nearly equal weight. To be truly effective, the reversals must balance each other.

As with other point-of-view-driven plots, the success of this kind of story depends on your making sure that the words or actions that are being mirrored are carefully chosen and supported. As an example, think about Charles Dickens' most famous ghost story, *A Christmas Carol*, in which Ebenezer Scrooge undergoes a major reversal from an unsympathetic and mean-spirited character to a sympathetic and likeable one. Dickens emphasizes Scrooge's reversal by having him say opposite things about Christmas at the beginning and the end of the story, and by having him make a generous contribution to the Christmas charity that he had spurned in the beginning of the tale. The audience is set up for this change of heart by witnessing a series of increasingly emotional responses by Scrooge to the visiting Spirits. As his fear grows, so too does the audience's longing for a successful outcome to the story.

Here is my example of a reversal narrative, a story of a summer camp romance gone awry.

The Rabbit

One afternoon while they were waiting for the
camp boat that would take them to the island to arrive,
she suggested that they take a walk. And since he was
infatuated with her, attracted by her good looks and
teasing sexuality, he readily agreed. The golden sunlight
poured through the summer pines like warmed butter as
they walked the path. A soft breeze carried the scent of
wildflowers and the sounds of the insect industry from the
green heart of the forest. When they came to the clearing,
they stopped and fell into each other's arms on a bed of
white clover blossoms.

Their kisses began slowly, but, fueled by wanting,
soon grew passionate, hungry for the mysteries behind
lips and teeth. Then the rabbit came into the clearing.
It leapt out of the dark undergrowth of brush, arching
up through the sunlight before gravity pulled it back to
earth. It landed with a soft thud, and the rabbit's muscles
bunched and propelled it skyward again, over them, so
close that he could feel the heat of the rabbit, the brush
of its fur, as it sailed past. He turned away from her kiss
to watch as it struck the ground and leapt again, out of
sight, into the shadowy folds of the leafy green curtain.

What would make a rabbit do that? He looked back.
Nothing followed. Nothing could be seen where the rabbit
had entered the clearing.

She asked what was happening. He told her about the
rabbit and, with a single stupid gesture, showed her how
it moved. She laughed. He repeated the gesture until she
stopped laughing and pulled him close. They returned to
the kissing. But it was not the same.

He suggested that it was time to go to back. The
boat would be waiting, and he got up. She got up with a
chorus of reluctant protests, but he did not hear her. He
had gone over to look at the spot where the rabbit had
been. Pushing back the green flags of resplendent nature,
he saw nothing. No track, no scent, no form, no spore.
Yet he sensed that there was something there, just beyond

reach, something there in the forest, patient and watching.

As they walked back to the landing, she complained that summer camp was making her fat, but he was not listening. His eyes, like frightened birds, flew from branch to branch, finding no comfort in the failing light that fell through holes in the dark canopy of needles. A cold wind carried the scent of decay, mushrooms, and rotting wood. All the while, his head was turned, listening for the soft step of whatever followed on the dry leaves, for the snap of a branch that would signal something was close by.

When they got to the dock, the others were waiting. She told them about the rabbit and showed them the funny gesture. Everyone laughed as they loaded their gear. He said nothing. He got in the boat and looked longingly towards the island cabins and the lazy clouds sailing a watery blue sky. Maybe it would be different once they were docked, but while they crossed the lake, the darkness came out of the forest. It followed them across open water and settled within him.

The structure in this story is very simple: a single incident changes the way in which the environment is interpreted by a character in the story and by the audience as well. The shift is marked by the simple descriptions of the way the forest looks before and after: from buttery sunlight to failing light, and from a fragrant bounty to the rot of decay. The shift is enough to propel the story forward, to provide the discomfort that offsets the romance in this small tale, to give motive to the unexpected action that breaks the romantic spell, and to move the audience from one kind of anticipation to another.

An important thing to think about is who is telling the story. When told in the first person, is the mirroring something that the character is aware of, or is it something only the audience is aware of? When a reversal plot is crafted in the third person, it is easier to set up the shifts because the narrator stands outside of the tale, but even then the question of whether the characters are conscious of the change will apply.

With the oral story, the audience does not have the luxury of being able to go back to read a passage a second time, which necessitates that the reversal must be very clear. The audience must be able to compare "X0" to "0X" to understand what the mirroring elements are. If you choose to mirror physical description, you have to emphasize the physical in both the "before" and "after" segments of the story. If you choose emotional feelings, you have to demonstrate how the character undergoing the change felt before in order for the audience to recognize how the feeling is mirrored afterward.

In a written narrative, the reader can go back and look at the descriptions and details, but that does not relieve you of the obligation to provide clarity. If anything, because the reader can examine the before and after, it necessitates a greater care in showing what changes for the characters without telling readers how they are to feel about those changes.

On the simplest level, if you chart out the narrative progression and mark where you want the shift to occur before you begin construction of the story proper, it makes building the story easier. Is the mirroring physical or emotional, conveyed by action or character? It is explicit in the story or implicit in the way the audience understands or feels about the story? Then, in the crafting of the material, you can check the details and action against your charting to keep yourself on track.

In structuring the reversal narrative, you have to know how you are going to shift the way the audience feels about or understands a character or a situation. More importantly, you have to know why you want to do so. Respect the readers and listeners: make them your partners in understanding what the story means. There is no point in using the mirroring technique if it does not deepen or move the story forward and provide a richer, more nuanced way to understand the world the characters live in.

Exercises

1. Think about a story you want to tell using a reversal plot. What will change over the course of the story? The way we understand a character? Behavior? The meaning of a particular decision or action? Using a set of three-by-five cards, put the "before" on one card and the "after" on another. If, as an example, the "before" is that the character is cowardly, how is that expressed? Then ask yourself what the mirror image of that would be and put that on the "after" card. Do not worry if the "before" and "after" seem crude and obvious, because at this stage they are the building blocks of a story, not the finished story itself.

Decide how many mirrored images you need for this story. Two? Three or more? On another set of cards, note the rough narrative progression, and set those cards out in order. Decide where the various "before" and "after" cards should be placed along that narrative progression and put them there.

Tell or write that first draft version of the story. What needs to be worked on? Are the items that you want to mirror in the right places? Is there an engaging emotional arc that lets the readers or audience members shift their perceptions of what is happening and what it means? Where do you need to add material to make smooth transitions or set the scene?

Write or tell a second version of the story, paying particular attention to the descriptive language. Remember that the use of descriptive adjectives and telling detail is very helpful in creating what the reader or audience imagines and feels. Appeal to the senses. You know how the story ends, but the reader or listener does not, so don't telegraph what is coming. Demonstrate what happens rather than explain what happens. Show how the villain was redeemed or the good girl went bad. Let the audience members appreciate that what they thought was right or true has given way to another, deeper understanding of how the world or the human heart works.

2. Think of a time when you changed your opinion about something—a person, food, event, or perhaps yourself. Looking at the change, how would you describe the "before"? What was said or done? How would you use a description of the time and place to

express how you felt? What caused the change? Did you initiate the change, or did someone or something else? How would you describe the "after"? What was said or done that demonstrated the change? You now have the bare bones of a mirror story. Flesh it out, and share it with someone. What does that person like? What questions does he or she have? What does that person want more of? Considering the responses, decide what you will do to polish this story.

Rewrite or retell it with an eye towards having everything work together to move the reader or listener through your experience of changing your opinion.

CHAPTER NINE

FULL CIRCLE

"The only rule for going into a flashback is to avoid confusing the reader."
Ayn Rand

Circular Plot, Variation One: Flashback

Formula: D-A-B-C-D-End
Focus: Time progression
Book or movie: *Alice in Wonderland*
                  Big Fish

The circular plot form is most commonly told as a "flashback" in which we begin at a particular point in time and then go back to some earlier moment, only to return through the narrative to the point of departure. In the movies, the flashback often begins at the moment of death or a point of extreme crisis. Examples include Charles Foster Kane whispering "Rosebud" to begin *Citizen Kane*, or Jeff Bridges, as the English professor in the remake of *D.O.A.*, stumbling into the police station to announce a murder, his murder. That dramatic moment often is followed by the cliché of the scene wiggling or blurring, and we are then magically whisked back in time to see the story of how we got to the dramatic moment.

It also is possible to tell circular narratives in which we progress *forward* from a point of departure and return to that starting point at the end. The most obvious example I can think of is *Alice in Wonderland* or the famous season of the television show *Dallas* in which it become clear at the conclusion of the year that the whole season had "all been a dream." I'll leave you to decide whether the flashback is an overused plot form, but it is worth learning how to do it successfully. Here is *Jack* as a flashback:

> Jack holds the axe as the Giant comes tumbling down
> with a tangle of green beanstalk wrapped around his
> fist. Jack remembers how it all began: a day that started
> like any day—hungry. There was nothing to eat in the

house, and so he could not argue with Mother that it was time for desperate action. He didn't want to sell the skinny cow and that might explain the bad bargain he made. Or maybe he had actually believed that they were magic beans. How naive was he, or how desperate, that he actually planted them in hopes that they would produce a miracle? A miracle indeed—he was as surprised as Mother was when they sprouted.

The thing about miracles is that they require faith, and there was plenty of that in the dizzy ascent into the clouds. More than once he told himself, "Don't look down, move forward, forward towards whatever comes next."

He knows now that next was not simply the Giant's house in the mist and his fearful knocking at the door. That was simple curiosity. The door opened and the unexpected was the maternal welcome of the wife, with her smothering hospitality and solicitous kindness. He had been spoon-deep in the bowl of savory broth as the Giant returned with the fearful announcement of "Fee, fi, fo, fum!"

Jack still cannot understand why she helped him. Why she hid him in the cupboard and distracted the Giant with coy gestures and flirtatious talk, all the while looking at the cupboard. He knew enough to run when he could and take the bag of gold on the way out. But there was something unfinished in that kitchen, the love of the moth for the flame, perhaps, in his wanting to see her again. The scene repeated itself, but this time her fussing seemed more purposeful, more suggestive of intent. Inside the cupboard, Jack wondered, was the dress she wore more revealing of her ample bosom?

Jack could understand the Giant's anger as he stole a second time. The rattling of the heavens was like thunder, but what should have been lesson enough, he now understood, was wasted on him. Had he been addicted to the fear or to the kindness? The final straw was the harp crying out. There was no pretense in that moment, and he saw the look of expectation or pleasure on the wife's face as he raced out the open door with the Giant behind. It was a wild chase through the clouds, towards the thin, green tendrils of the beanstalk. Equally wild was the descent, Jack confident in repetition and the Giant tentative on the living vine. He was set up for a fall. Jack knew what he had to do, and he imagined that she knew as well. Perhaps she did not know precisely what the means would be, but the desired outcome was certain. She would be freed of that man at last.

Now it's over. The beanstalk lies like a tangled rope around the body of the Giant, and Jack's mother is running towards him with her arms outstretched. Jack looks up to the heavens and wishes the newly widowed well.

On one level, a flashback is nothing more than a long digression, giving us background about the significance or value of a critical moment in the story. In most examples, the story begins with a physical, emotional, or psychological crisis that grabs the audience's or reader's attention. Once that attention is gained—once the audience is sympathetic—the flashback's primary purpose is to explain how we arrived at this moment.

The key to successfully creating a flashback is to understand why you are going back and how far is sufficient to allow you to present the information that the audience really needs for the story. Think of the movie *Big Fish*, which uses many flashbacks to give us pieces of the story and does not try to weave them into a whole until the end, when the truth of the various remembered stories is confirmed.

Here is an example of a flashback narrative that I created in the style of a folk tale. It is set in a nameless country in either the present or the not-too-distant past.

Pablito Bueno

On the outskirts of a village so small it was but a handful of stone houses clinging to the shadow of the mountainside, Guillermo saw a crowd surging towards a rundown church. He joined them and pushed his way

*past the abandoned crutches hanging by the door, into
the darkness, into clouds of sweet incense and murmured
supplications filling the sanctuary. Then Guillermo
saw it, a tattered whalebone corset hanging on the wall,
illuminated by the flicker of dozens of votive candles.
Someone else might wonder how such a profane object
could be venerated as a religious icon, but Guillermo
knew and felt his knees buckle. It was not piety or the
sight of the corset that made him tremble, but what he had
come to claim beneath the corset: his long-departed father.*

*His father's name was Pablito Bueno, though there
was nothing "ito," nothing endearing or little about this
"Pablo," nor any good in this "Bueno." A tall man of
great strength, great riches, great rage, he was a man who
would not be denied. He had purchased a wife from a poor
family fallen on hard times, who bore him three children
and died of shame. After that, a locked iron gate kept out
what he could not control and kept in all that he could.
His dark eyes cherished what he had and dammed what he
could not have.*

*After her death, he wore a whalebone corset, not from
vanity or to hold in his sagging flesh, but for the pleasure
he felt when one of the daughters would place her knee
against his back to brace herself as she pulled with all her
might to tighten the laces.*

*A man of certain obsessions, he once found a piece of
colored lint in his belly button. He put it in a small jar,
labeled it with the day and date, and set it on a shelf. Soon
it was joined by other bits of himself—fingernail and toe
nail clippings, ear wax—all meticulously saved in small
jars that were labeled with the day and month. The jars
slowly displaced the books in the library, filling the nooks
and crannies of the house with his dead skin.*

*He turned his attention to the children, entering their
rooms while they were sleeping to pull back the sheets,
tenderly holding their beautiful feet in one hand and a
golden shears in the other. Snip, snip, and then he would
take away the clippings. The sisters grew afraid and*

turned to their brother, Guillermo, for help. Be patient, he
counseled—he had a plan.

One day, Pablito watched as Guillermo walked
barefoot across a room. His toenails were long, curved,
and painted black, like the claws of a wild animal. Pablito
could barely wait for the boy to go to bed before he took the
golden scissors in his shaking hands and went down the
hall. As he reached out to pull back the sheet, the pistol
kept under Guillermo's pillow came out and expelled a
single shot. The bullet entered the center of the father's
forehead, and the old man fell back in a fountain of blood.

In the darkest hour of night, the children carried
Pablito Bueno out of the house and placed him in the
street. But that was not all. They scurried back and forth
like ants, emptying the shelves, placing armfuls of jars
around the body and along the curb. When they were
done, they went in, locked the gate, and waited for the
authorities to arrive.

A man with a horse and cart came down the street
and stopped to look at the body. To his surprise, the dead
man sat up. When he asked who this bleeding man was,
the strange figure shrugged and offered to buy the cart.
No fool, the man sold the cart but kept the horse and went
on his way as Pablito loaded the jars into the cart, put
himself where the horse used to be, and turned towards
sunrise.

When Guillermo discovered the body was gone, he
assumed the police had removed it, but no one came to
make inquiries or inform them of the sad news of their
father's tragic end. As the days and weeks passed, the
seed of fear that Pablito wasn't dead after all but would
come back to deliver a terrible revenge grew in every
corner of the cold house. But he did not come back, and
over the course of years, a longing to know where their
father had gone leached away the bitter memory of the
jars and golden scissors. A thorny hedge took root around
Guillermo's heart, pricking his conscience and sending
him out to wander the streets, the newspaper offices, and

dusty archives of civic buildings in search of the answer.

He crossed fields and searched forests, visited ever-further villages before he came across a man in whose house was a glass jar with toenail clippings set on a shelf with votive lights on each side. Guillermo stared in amazement as the man told him that these were the relics of his favorite holy saint, Ignatius, which the peddler with a hole in his head had sold him some years ago. Guillermo could not persuade the man that it was a fraud, nor would the man sell him the jar marked with day, month, year, and tiny crescent yellow moons inside.

That discovery was enough to lead Guillermo from one poor village to the next. At each stop, he heard the stories of the peddler who sold the relics of the saints to people who believed with all their hearts that relics bartered for a thin coin or, sometimes, a crust of bread contained a blessing. Finally, in a village half way to tomorrow, he was told that seven pilgrims were about to leave to see the peddler himself. It was said that he could cure the sick, make the lame walk, bring the dead back to life if your faith was strong enough. Guillermo parted with his last coins and sat on the back of a donkey as it tread the unmapped path over the black mountains.

Now he stood above the prostrate throng before the peddler himself. Guillermo rushed to the altar and took the skull polished with the kisses of the faithful in his hands. It had a hole in the middle, and, as Guillermo turned it over, the bullet inside rolled a little song of recognition. At last he had truly found Pablito Bueno— father, monster, charlatan, confessor, and saint, all at once. Guillermo wept, asking Heaven for forgiveness, and as he did, the thorny thicket choking his heart fell away, the red rose of peace blooming in its place.

Here are some questions that are worth asking about the flashback: Does it add interest to the story? Is it necessary? Will one do, or do you need several in order to show different aspects of characters or situations? How much is left to tell after the flashback is finished? Is there still a lot to say, or does the story come to a swift end after we have resolved the crisis?

I cannot emphasize enough the value of thinking through and making conscious choices about how you structure the flashback. This narrative form can be told in the first, second, or third person, and in the present or past tense. The choice of voice and tense will go a long way in determining the way the flashback will be structured. What I want to reinforce now is the simple but critical understanding that the decision to use a flashback should—say it with me—move the entire story forward, inviting the audience members into the world of the story and making them care about what happens next.

Circular Plot, Variation Two: String of Pearls

Formula: Any ordering of a set, such as D-C-E-B-A-End, or
                B–D–A–E-C-End
Focus: Point of view
Book or movie: Kurt Vonnegut's *Slaughterhouse Five*

The string of pearls is another version of the circular plot form. It is circular not in the sense that we are brought back to a certain point in time, like in a flashback, but in the sense that the story consists of a series of vignettes arranged like a string of pearls decorating the graceful neck of a theme. In a string-of-pearls story, you can begin at *any* point, tell the tale either forward or backward, and have it contain the same meaning. Continuing with the metaphor of the pearl necklace, each pearl may be examined in detail, with its own peculiarities, shading, and variations contributing to the whole. Each pearl must be able to stand alone. Think about Kurt Vonnegut's *Slaughterhouse Five* with Billy Pilgrim jumping back and forth in time. You can read the chapters in any order and still have a thoroughly satisfying experience.

Because this story can be assembled in any order, this is a plot form that presumes the audience's intelligence and a fairly high degree of trust between the creator and those receiving the story. Whatever through-line may be found in this narrative pattern is established by those in the audience as they assemble the story in their heads. They do so by moving from one vignette to another, making what they will of the relationship of the elements and the sequence in which they are being told. The audience makes the story a complete experience, establishing a meaning from the implicit theme presented. Think of it as a narrative crossword puzzle in which you present the clues, and audience members draw their conclusions as to what it is and what it means.

This form of circular story often gains power from being retold, with each retelling letting the audience enter at a different starting point and taking them to a different ending point as well. This act of repetition serves two functions: first, it provides a different storytelling experience for those in the audience, one that allows them to hear different facets or relationships with each telling. Second, the repetition also allows the teller to subtly shift the focus of the story with each telling, emphasizing different ways of interpreting the material without changing the central meaning of the story. If the function of a flashback is to take us from one moment back or forward in time only to return to our starting point, the function of a string of pearls is to let us compare and contrast various moments within a story without having to enter and exit at the same point of the story.

Here is a circular tale from my repertoire that uses this string-of-pearls approach. This story is performed as a prose poem, verbal jazz if you will, with the emphasis on tonality and imagery. I'll present it in two variations so you can see the effect of ordering. The first time, I tell it with the segments ordered I–II–III–IV. In the second telling, the segments are ordered II–IV–III–I.

Making Chili (a)

(I) *A breeze stirred in South Dakota and got a notion to travel. It swept over the sunbaked plain, tickling the wild grasses, and across the ordered farm fields. It caressed the green stalks of corn. It crossed the low, rolling Iowa hills and skittered into Minnesota. It slid past Blue Earth and Rochester, curled around a burr oak near the Wiscoy Valley, then slid along the bluffs. It fluttered the curtains of the farmhouse overlooking the Mississippi Valley. It circled the warm kitchen like a restless cat and lifted the rich scent of simmering chili from the black pot that stood on the stove. Hmmm, it smelled sooooo good.*

(II) Gregory and I were in town when the undeniable urge came. Let's have chili for supper. Real chili the color of red mud, thick with chunks of meat, onion, and lots of hot peppers.

"Yah," he says, "that sounds like a winner with some crusty bread. Yes, that sounds good."

Oh, it's good? You want good? Here's good that will bring tears to your eyes. A big bowl of spicy, hot chili with a toasted slice of crusty sourdough bread topped with a thick slab of butter and a cold beer on the side. You know, with the glass taken right out of the freezer, the golden balm of joy poured over the iced rim, the amber settling below a white head of fine bubbles as thick as snow. Now there is a meal worth suffering for. There is a meal to make your tongue jump and your taste buds work overtime.

(III) Take the black skillet, and set it on the flame. Put in a stab of—well, purists would use lard—but you can use olive oil or canola or any grease just as well. Add the meat. A pound or two is about right. Beef, pork, lamb, venison, rattlesnake—anything will do.

I knew a guy who was partial to squirrel, but it is a little stringy for my taste. I even heard of certain unhappy places where rat chili is real popular. Man, we had some rats in the barn that were big enough to be considered, but when it comes right down to it, I prefer beef: cheap chuck steak, sometimes round, but really any tough bit of old bossy that will be improved with a couple of hours of simmering. That was what I used when I first learned the wonder of making the Devil's due, and, as we know, it's the Texas standard.

Trim all but about 1/8th of an inch of fat. Cut into chunks—about the size of the tip of your thumb—and throw them in with the smashed-up garlic. Hell, use two or three heads. Don't be shy. The garlic is just the start of the happy mouth dance. For the chili I am thinking of, there can hardly be too much garlic, for its deep, resonant flavor must balance the pure sizzle of the chilies. Turn up the heat to sear the meat. Meanwhile, chop an onion into big pieces. Toss them into the skillet. Toss in a pinch of cumin and a couple pinches of oregano, some black pepper. Let the onions simmer until translucent. Empty the skillet with the browned meat, garlic, and onions into a good-sized kettle or stew pot. Add a couple of inches of actual tomato, not sauce. You can use peeled, stewed, sliced, diced, or whole tomatoes. They are background music, not the melody, so don't go and do what so many sissy cooks do, making the pot a sea of watery red.

Add the chopped chilies. Add a half bottle of beer. Add cider or balsamic vinegar if you've got a hankering. Add chocolate. Add molasses. Add mushrooms. Add all those secret ingredients years of experimentation and lack of good sense have lead you to believe are necessary for a truly distinguished chili. Add anything, except beans, for you and me both know that beans are to real chili what sin is to the preacher—an abomination to be shunned, the source of damnation, and that which must be repented of.

Cook the whole mess for a couple of hours. Cook it to the density of mud and the color of old rust, until the flavor fuses, and you can't stand looking at it any longer. Then dig in.

(IV) I am chopping fire. It is good. The knife blade glows with the essence of heat. It is the fine, clear fire on the inside that makes one chili the Fourth of July and another oak logs at Christmas. Don't be afraid. I'm not. Let me sing praise for the mighty chili pepper. There are twelve fat, green Jalapenos on the cutting board. When the knife blade splits the skin, drum head tight, there is an audible pop. Inside the seeds shine. Mix them with the mild, finger-length Anaheims or purists turn away, or Banana peppers the color of yellow-waxed fruit. Or do a few lipstick-red Serranos, glowing like the tail lights of a '59 Cadillac. Oh baby—we're cruising tonight. When I want my mouth to curse me, but my belly to dwell with the long, slow burn of having cooked up a few yellow Scotch Bonnets, it is like the kerosene hiss of the old lamp

*and a pure act of the will. In spring, when the road is
mud and the fields hunger for green, I'll use the old fire
of dark-red Anchos, the leathery slices like dried blood,
anticipating the simmering pot — oh, how they bloat in the
bubbling juices, renewing their abiding heat. Short or fat,
long or thin, let me praise this purifying heat, and wash
my hands twice after handling those sacred fires.*

Here is the second variation, based on a recorded telling with
performance instructions added in parentheses:

Making Chili (b)

(II) (Say in a cool, slow voice) *Gregory and I were
in town when the undeniable urge came. Let's have chili
for supper. Real spicy chili the color of red mud, thick with
chunks of meat, onion, and lots of hot peppers.*

(Second voice—slow) *"Yah"," he says, "that
sounds like a winner with some crusty bread. Yes, that
sounds good."*

(Pickup speed as you say the following) *Oh, it's
good? You want good? Here's good that will bring tears
to your eyes. A big bowl of spicy,* (vocal emphasis on
the underlined) <u>*hot*</u> *chili with a toasted slice of crusty
sourdough bread topped with a thick slab of butter and
a* (vocal emphasis on the underlined) <u>*cold*</u> *beer on
the side. You know, with the glass taken right out of the
freezer, the golden balm of joy poured over the iced rim,
the amber settling below a white head of fine bubbles as
thick as snow. Now there is a meal worth suffering for.
There is a meal to make your tongue* (vocal emphasis
on the underlined) <u>*jump*</u> *and your taste buds work
overtime.*

(IV) (say in a lyrical style) *I am chopping fire. It
is good. The knife blade glows with the essence of heat.
It is the fine, clear fire on the inside that makes one chili
the Fourth of July and another oak logs at Christmas.
Don't be afraid.* (whisper the following) *I'm not.* (use
full voice for the following) *Let me sing praise for the*

mighty chili pepper. There are twelve fat, green Jalapenos on the cutting board. When the knife blade splits the skin, drum head tight, there is an audible pop. Inside the seeds shine. Mix them with the mild finger length Anaheims or purists turn away, or Banana peppers the color of yellow-waxed fruit. Or do a few lipstick-red Serranos, glowing like the tail lights of a '59 Cadillac. (vocal emphasis on the underlined) *Oh baby—we're cruising tonight. When I want my mouth to curse me, but my belly to dwell with the long, slow burn of having cooked up a few yellow Scotch Bonnets, it is like the kerosene hiss of the old lamp and* (say the underlined slowly) *a pure act of the will. In spring, when the road is mud and the fields hunger for green, I'll use the old fire of dark-red Anchos, the leathery slices like dried blood, anticipating the simmering pot.* (vocal emphasis on the underlined) *O, how they bloat in the bubbling juices, renewing their abiding heat. Short or fat, long or thin, let me praise this purifying heat, and wash my hands twice after handling those sacred fires.*

(III) (Quickly, using the asides like horn solos) *Take the black skillet, and set it on the flame. Put in a stab of—well, purists would use lard—but you can use olive oil or canola or any grease just as well. Add the meat. A pound or two is about right. Beef, pork, lamb, venison, rattlesnake—anything will do.*

(Say the following softly, like you're telling a secret) *I knew a guy who was partial to squirrel, but it is a little stringy for my taste. I even heard of certain unhappy places where rat chili is real popular. Man, we had some rats in the barn that were big enough to be considered,* (return to basic tempo vocal level) *but when it comes right down to it, I prefer beef: cheap chuck steak, sometimes round, but really any tough bit of old bossy that will be improved with a couple of hours of simmering. That was what I used when I first learned the wonder of making the Devil's due, and, as we know, it's the Texas standard.*

Trim all but about 1/8th of an inch of fat. Cut into

chunks —about the size of the tip of your thumb —and
throw them in with the smashed-up garlic. Hell, use two
or three heads. Don't be shy. The garlic is just the start
of the happy mouth dance. For the chili I am thinking of,
there can hardly be too much garlic, for its deep, resonant
flavor must balance the pure sizzle of the chilies. Turn
up the heat to sear the meat. Meanwhile, chop an onion
into big pieces. Toss them into the skillet. Toss in a pinch
of cumin and a couple pinches of oregano, some black
pepper. Let the onions simmer until translucent. Empty
the skillet with the browned meat, garlic, and onions into
a good-sized kettle or stew pot. Add a couple of inches
of actual tomato, not sauce. You can use peeled, stewed,
sliced, diced, or whole tomatoes. They are (emphasize
the underlined slowly and then quicken the pace for
the remaining text) *background music, not the melody,*
so don't go and do what so many sissy cooks do, making
the pot a sea of watery red.

(Return to basic vocal tempo) *Add the chopped*
chilies. Add a half bottle of beer. Add cider or balsamic
vinegar if you've got a hankering. Add chocolate.
Add molasses. Add mushrooms. Add all those secret
ingredients years of experimentation and lack of good
sense have lead you to believe are necessary for a truly
distinguished chili. Add anything (vocal emphasis on
the underlined as a series of emphasized beats—as
in a song with a great hook, they are keeping time
for the telling) *except beans. Yes, say it again, except*
beans, for you and me both know that (say the following
underlined parts with a rising voice) *beans are to real*
chili what sin is to the preacher —an abomination to be
shunned, a source of damnation and that which must be
repented of. (Shout out) *Lord have mercy!*

Just cook, I say it again, (vocal emphasis on the
underlined words in this paragraph) *cook the whole*
mess for a couple of hours. Cook it to the density of mud
and the color of old rust. Until the flavor fuses, and you
can't stand looking at it any longer. Then dig in. Then

put it away and let it <u>age for a day</u>. Bring it back and <u>heat</u> it again! <u>Serve</u> it up and <u>say</u> your prayers. A good chili is the <u>true</u> forbidden fruit, the (vocal emphasis on the underlined) <u>manna</u> *from Heaven, and the best there is gives you a <u>tongue</u> of fire and a <u>burning in</u> your belly.*

(I) (Say softly) *A breeze stirred in South Dakota and got a notion to travel. It swept over the sunbaked plain, tickling the wild grasses, and across the ordered farm fields. It caressed the green stalks of corn. It crossed the low, rolling Iowa hills and skittered into Minnesota. It slid past Blue Earth and Rochester, curled around a burr oak near the Wiscoy Valley, then slid along the bluffs. It fluttered the curtains of the farmhouse overlooking the Mississippi Valley. It circled the warm kitchen like a restless cat and lifted the rich scent of simmering chili from the black pot that stood on the stove.* (slowly emphasize the underlined) <u>*Hmmm, it smelled sooooo good.*</u>

Since each segment of this story has a distinct weight and presence, I usually try to choose a point of entry and sequence the segments in a way that invites the audience into the emotional power of the images. If the audience members are ready for humor, I might begin with the "chili recipe" segment (III) that lends itself to laughter. If the mood is quieter, more meditative, a better place to begin is the "a breeze stirred in South Dakota and got a notion to travel" segment (I).

The circular, string-of-pearls plot depends on the development of the individual vignettes as complete and emotionally satisfying. For a true string of pearls, each vignette must be specific, must have a compelling image, and must have an emotional tone, but it does not need to carry the full weight of the narrative. They can be quite diverse in focus and subject matter but must relate in some way to the larger theme. You can use any point of view, any tense, jumping from one to another as you move from segment to segment. The important thing is that at the conclusion, the audience feels that every segment of the story is necessary and gives us a greater understanding of the theme.

In some cases you may want to extemporaneously add segments, or drop segments. To help make that decision, I would encourage you to practice telling many different sequences and observe how various audiences respond to the different combinations.

It doesn't get any more post-modern and deconstructed than this in the oral tradition. This is the strength and the weakness of both the string-of-pearls and the list (which we will get to next) narrative forms: they offer both more freedom and more risk than traditional narrative progressions. It is a freedom that can produce very good stories provided you are willing to do the work.

Exercises

1. Let's create a flashback. Begin by deciding what story you want to tell. For the purposes of this exercise, use a folk or fairy tale you know rather than a personal story. *Little Red Riding Hood* or *Three Little Pigs* would be good options.

Decide where in the story you want to insert a flashback. As an example, you might want to insert a flashback into *Little Red Riding Hood* at the point where the girl meets the wolf in Grandma's bed. You now have a couple of options. The first is to place the bed scene and the flashback at the beginning of the story and have everything that came before the bed scene be part of the flashback—going back to Mother telling Little Red Riding Hood to take the basket of goodies to Grandma. In this choice, the flashback is set at the decisive moment when there is the most at stake and must demonstrate the building tension that makes this the decisive moment.

The second option is to tell the story much like a straight narrative and insert the flashback not at the beginning but well into the story, when the girl sees the Wolf in Grandma's bed. In this option, the flashback would contain a smaller, critical chunk of the story—perhaps the part when the girl meets the Wolf in the woods—that had been withheld. In this option, the flashback functions similarly to a revelation plot.

Once you have decided which use of the flashback suits your story, write or tell it. Is the finished story satisfying? Does the flashback heighten the tension, or provide us with a greater understanding of who, what, where, when, or why? If it does not, you should decide whether that weakness is because the flashback is in the wrong place or because you do not need it to begin with. Remember, the function of a flashback is to deepen our understanding of the story.

2. Now, let's try a string of pearls. Pick a topic or theme for an original story, perhaps the story of an accident or a significant event in a person's life. You want to create a multifaceted story in which you can use the advantages of the string-of-pearls format. Taking a set of three-by-five cards, write your notes and images (with one

critical image or action on each card) for the following vignettes that
might appear in a string-of-pearls narrative:

a. A vignette told from a first-person point of view.
b. A vignette describing time and / or place.
c. A vignette in the third person describing an interaction
    between two characters.
d. A vignette that is poetic or philosophical in tone.
e. A vignette set in the present tense.
f. A vignette set in the past tense.

These are the bare bones of the story. Flesh out each vignette,
paying attention to descriptive language. Because a string of pearls is
as much about what is not said—the central theme or the true subject
of the story—try to be sensitive to how each vignette suggests (but
does not give away) the theme.

Shuffle the cards, place them face down, and pull a card from the
top of the pile. Write or tell that vignette. Pick up the next card and
repeat the process until you have used every card. What was that
story? Was it satisfying or do you need to add material to fill in gaps
and enrich the emotional quality? If so, add those cards to the pile.

Shuffle the pile a second time and repeat the process. If you
are doing this exercise in a group, you can have each person take
a turn shuffling and using the cards. Make a game of it. What do
people keep from another's version and what unique take does each
person provide using the same set of bare-bones cards? Have the
group track the order of each telling to see whether particular orders
are more satisfying than others. Have the group vote or come to a
consensus on which telling best captured the theme.

CHAPTER TEN

MAKING A LIST

"The human animal differs from the lesser primates in his passion for 'Ten Best' lists."

H. Allen Smith

The List Plot

Formula: One-Two-Three-Four-Five (or any set of items)-End
Focus: Point of view
Book or movie: Leslie Marmon Silko's *Storyteller*
               Thirty Two Short Films about Glenn Gould

Of all the narrative plot forms that I use in crafting personal stories, the list story is my favorite. It is a thing of beauty, a narrative progression that is particularly suited for use with difficult or seemingly unwieldy material. Got something so big you don't know where to begin? Make a list. Want to sort out the essential story, or tease out multiple aspects of a theme? Use a list.

In its simplest form, the list story, like a string of pearls, uses a series of stand-alone vignettes to present content organized around some common theme. Unlike a string of pearls, it has specific characteristics. First, it is organized around a specific set of related items. It could be grouped as a set of numbers (one through seven, as an example), or a set of colors, directions, days, or the kinds of cars you've owned, etc. One list story I tell, called *Seven Things I Know about the Mississippi River,* is organized around geographic features of the river. The example from my repertoire that I include later in this chapter is organized around the seasons of the year, with vignettes about saunas in winter, spring, summer, and fall. Secondly, while the vignettes in a string-of-pearls story can be randomly ordered, a list story works best when it adheres to a formula, one of which I will outline below.

The number of items included in a list is determined by how many vignettes are needed to tell the story or the ability of an audience to follow the thread. The late Spaulding Gray used to tell a story about every theater performance he had appeared in. When I saw it, there were thirty-two vignettes, the longest of which took about ten minutes to tell and the shortest of which was a single sentence. Frankly, the longer the list, the more pressure there is on the teller to use shorter vignettes to keep the audience engaged. For writers, this is less of an issue because the reader always can go back and reread the list.

In creating a list story, it often is helpful to operate within a formula. The one I and others have used with great success holds that for any list story you create, there should be at least four items. The first item will introduce the subject or set the emotional tone. The second or third item is humorous, reassuring people in the audience that this will be something they can relate to. The next-to-the-last item carries the emotional weight, and the last one resolves the theme. Here is an example of the formula as a prose poem:

Some Things I Know
(about Sewing Machines and Sperm)

1. *The old-fashioned machine had a cast-iron treadle, a stiff tradition handed down from some distant grandmother, dragged from the closet, set before the window, and commanded to its singular task. It set to work remaking the world.*

2. *To fulfill their promise, the mighty swimmers found a hole in the dam and swam on. Far, silent, lonely in their singular duty, one of them continued to the waiting welcome shore.*

3. *In and out, in and out, the happy needle was stitching something. "I'm pregnant," she said. In his surprise, the finger remained in the needle's path, in and out. Pulling the pricked finger away with a trail of bloody thread like an umbilical cord, he said, "In fairy tales, this would be a bad omen."*

4. *Afterwards, it was all put away or given away. The booties, blankets, the little pillow that had cradled the baby's head, and that hulking repudiation of iron-willed purpose with them, cast back into the dark closet. The very sound of in and out, in and out —a reminder of all*

that was undone.

*5. The sewing machine waits in the dark, while
moonlight fills the hollow of the room. For ten long years
they wept, as legion upon legion of swimmers were set to
the task; and though the dams are gone, not one arrived
upon the long-sought shore.*

The first vignette introduces the subject or emotional tone, and
invites the audience into the story. One of the nice things about list
stories is that you can be quite lyrical, loading the first item with
imagery to declare to the audience, "This is not your classic folk
tale." In this example, I begin with the image of the sewing machine
brought out of the closet.

The second or third item in the list should be humorous. There is
a reason for this. Simply put, once the audience members realize that
it is not your standard plot form, they want to know that there are
still places in this story that are familiar and comforting, so let them
have a laugh. There is always a laugh when the audience connects
the image of the "swimmers" to the "sperm" of the title and, often,
another laugh at the "bad omen" line in the third vignette.

The next-to-the-last item in a list story—no matter how long the
list might be—provides the emotional high point. Here is where the
meaning of the story is presented—a combination of point of view,
narrative progression, and emotional arc that provides the reader or
listener with the beating heart of the story. In this example, it is the
description of the aftermath of the baby's death.

The final image resolves the story and often relates in some
way to the opening image. In this example, it is a variation on the
first image that extends the emotional arc, and joins the sperm and
sewing machine elements of the title into a single, poetic image.

To give you another example of the formula, here's *Jack* as a list
story organized around various kinds of hunger:

*1. They were always hungry. From sunup to
sundown and all through the night, the first and last
thought was of food. It was not a when-do-we-eat hungry,
but the gnawing-pain-that-doesn't-go-away hungry. So
hungry he couldn't think straight, had given up hope,*

and resigned himself to wither like the grass after the first killing frost.

2. It seemed like a fair trade. The town was so far away, and the market filled with reminders of what you did not have. Coffee and beer, meat and potatoes, fruit—oh God—sweet plums and golden oranges. Beans were good. They filled you up. You could cook beans right away. You could eat tonight and go to bed with something in the belly. So beans it was, and if they were magic, maybe they would satisfy him tonight and there would be enough left for tomorrow.

3. Beans, beans, the musical fruit, the more you eat, the more you toot!! When he let the first one rip, it was like celestial trumpets sounding the Judgment Day, but it smelled like someone had opened the door to Hell's sulfurous fires. Hungry or not, his mother would have none of it and threw the rest of the beans out the window.

4. The wife was baking breads, rolls, something that smelled good. She offered him a piece of sweet cake, and he eagerly took it. He was still hungry enough to not heed her good advice until the footsteps were already on the stair and that other hungry one entered the room. He could taste the butter turning in his mouth as he hid and heard: "Fe, fi, fo, fum—I smell the blood of an Englishman. Be he alive or be he dead, I'll grind his bones to bake my bread."

5. First there was the gold, then the little goose, and finally the singer of songs. The gold was cold to the touch, and while it might buy many a meal, it did not ease his hunger. He thought only of the wife's sweet cakes and the scones dripping with honey. It was not until he heard the first dulcet notes of the harp dancing across the room that he forgot he ever had an empty belly. Here was something to truly fill you, something to satisfy the wanting for all the sweet things of life.

6. It is not always the belly. Once we've tasted pleasure, adventure, the forbidden, we savor it. We have tasted this good thing and lived, really lived as men,

standing proud and tall in our accomplishment of what
we've dared to do. His mouth watered at the thought of
possessing this treasure, another man's pride and joy, and
he put aside sense for nonsense, caution for recklessness.
Take her he did with her cries echoing through the rooms.
Let the blood of the one who would come after her be on
his hands. An axe can cut many things. Afterwards, he
would bury the evidence.

7. You could buy a lot of bread for a bag of gold, and
fat cows and woolly sheep and the fields for them to graze.
His belly finally satisfied, he knew if they weren't hungry
now, it was as much luck and pluck as any courage he had
mustered. Eat or be eaten was the rule of nature. He had
been as lucky as he was hungry. For once his story ends
as he would have it be: happily ever after was a feast with
musical accompaniment.

Another virtue of a list story is that it is very useful in developing raw material. Suppose you've got a big, messy story. How do you know where to begin, where to end, or what it is about? Working on it as a list story (with or without the use of a formula) will give you an opportunity to play with perspectives of time, place, and point of view to find the core of the story. Storyteller Nancy Donoval often testifies to the efficiency of using the list as a tool to find out what portions of the raw material she is shaping into a story "have juice," as she puts it.

Like the proverbial "to-do" list its name derives from, the list story is a great way to boil the content of a story down to the essentials. It gives you tremendous freedom about how and what to tell, and yet it is specifically focused on presenting only as much material as is absolutely necessary for the story.

Here is my sample of a list story that was constructed out of a series of anecdotal tales about saunas. In this version, I use one from my father and three from my experience, arranged around seasons of the year. I have three or four other sauna events I could substitute for these depending on the audience and the length of time I want the story to take. One of the values of the list story is that you can have multiple vignettes available, and then use what is appropriate for the circumstance in which you are presenting.

I should note that this example deviates from the formula in that the next-to-the-last image does not carry the emotional weight of the story. That is loaded into the first and last vignettes. Also, all four seasonal vignettes I tell have elements of humor and wry observation of human behavior.

Sauna Cycle
Cosmology

I am Finnish. Sumalina. Beset with all the cultural tics that mark the Finns. How do you recognize a Finnish extrovert? He looks at your shoes. Beset with the cultural boons that mark them as well. Love of good design, love of cell phones, willing to eat a lot of fish. I worship at the altar of the sauna. Ironic for a people so reticent about their emotions that the true national religion is getting naked, sitting in a small hot box, and then cooling off by rolling in the snow or jumping in a lake.

"Sau-na." "Not sa-na." Not one of those places found in some cities where women of a certain kind offer services of a certain kind. Not one of those places in hotels and gyms where you have to wear swimming suits in a closet as a small electric box casts off barely enough heat to warm muffins. Those are not saunas. They may be called saunas but they lack the essential elements of the real thing: Heat! Lots of it — preferably a wood-burning stove. And cold!! Lots of it — preferably outdoors.

The essentials of religion are embodied in the four elements: earth, air, fire, and water. Rocks piled on the top of a barrel stove, wood, the smell of birch or pine, burning hot, the air heated to 140, 160, 180 degrees. Water poured on the rocks transformed to steam, which rises up, crosses the ceiling. It wraps you in a blanket of warmth, opening your pores. The trapped residue of living—dirt, toxins—pushed out from the inside. Sweat dripping off your nose and face and fingertips. Soap up

*and rinse off, if that is your way. Use a birch bough to
lightly beat the flesh, quickening the blood. There are
as many preferences as there are naked bodies on the
benches. A wet heat followed by dry heat. A dry heat
finished off with steam. An even heat for washing and a
blast for the departure. So hot you sit with a wet rag on
your head saying nothing until every breath is a searing
knife, then open the door, and go out. Out to a shower,
or better yet, a sudden plunge to close the pores in a lake
or a snow bank. Even on a summer's day, it is cooler
outside than in. Then go back inside, soap, rinse, and
repeat.*

The Sauna in Summer

*My father was on a trip to Finland and joined some
guys fishing in the Baltic. Six guys in a boat for three
hours when suddenly the captain says, "Time to sauna."
The boat heads for a tiny speck of rock jutting up amid
the waves. There's nothing on it but a sauna. They take
their clothes off, go inside, and are sitting, talking, when
the door opens. It's the Russians. Come to join them with
a bottle of vodka in hand. Détente, perestroika. When
they are done, which means when the vodka is gone, they
all go out, put their clothes on, get in their boats, and go
their separate ways and back to fishing.*

The Sauna in Fall

*I'm sitting in the public sauna in Hibbing.
Upstairs in the suites—as they are called—families,
couples, whatever combination of sexes that you want
to get naked with go about their business in spartan
rooms rented by the hour. Today, I'm downstairs in the
"bullpen," in the big room with the men. Mostly old
men, their wizened flesh hanging on brittle bones, white
hair—what there is of it—matted on their foreheads. One
old guy is the "dipper"—he controls the frequency of the
tin dipper's travel from the bucket to the rocks. Another
one is the keeper of the conversation. He steers it to and*

from weather, sports, politics, and labor unions (this is
Hibbing for God's sake—half the guys in the room spent
their lives in the mines) with the same phrase—"how's
about them"—and then gets the hell out of the way as
they all have their say. I say little, and when I do, they
cut me off mid-sentence with "aww, wait till you're as
old as we are and then tell us how it is."

One guy wants a smoke. The others say, "Cripes,
Tommy, step outside." He opens the door, steps out,
lights up, and sits in a chair that props the door open so
he can keep up the conversation, until they all complain
that he's letting the heat out. Then he puts the cigarette
out, moves the chair out of the way, goes back in. They
have been at this ritual for twenty years. When one dies,
they leave an empty place for him on the bench. There are
six now, and from the looks of it, by the time I get to be
their age, I'll be sitting here all by myself.

The Sauna in Winter

I'm at Emil Jalonen's cabin in Brimson. The sauna
is a little, pink, tin-and- pressed-wood shack halfway
between the house and the place where the stream ponds.
We go start the fire and then march down to the ice-
covered pond. Chop a hole in the ice. It won't freeze over
before we go in. Just as the hole opens, we lose the axe.
"We'll have to dive for it when we come back," he says.

It is minus ten degrees, dark at 5:00 p.m., with a
thin snow falling when we enter the sauna. It is cold in
the changing room and toasty warm when we open the
door, enter, and slide onto the benches. We talk food and
politics while heating up. Finally, when the thermometer
reads 170, Emil says, "Let's go." Out the door and
down the snowy path to the pond, the steam rising
from our bodies. I am in front, first to the hole—a black
square—hesitate, turn to look at Emil charging down
the path behind me, and leap feet first. The moment my
feet enter the water, every fiber of consciousness in my
body says, "Oh, nooooooo!" Before I am waist deep,

my testicles have retreated, and my penis is following.
Under I go, my foot touching the bottom, feeling around
for the axe. Not for very long, though. I pop up like a
bobber, get out—no, more like shoot out—levitate in the
darkness, and step to the bank. Emil leaps in and seems
to disappear. The axe emerges like Excalibur—Arthur's
sword—held aloft, Emil following triumphantly.

We run back to the sauna. Repeat the heat. Do not
repeat the plunge into the water. The second time, we
are content to stand outside under the blanket of night
cloud, letting the snowflakes fall on our naked flesh.

The Sauna in Spring

I'm at Emil's house on Park Point, the long, sandy
spit appended to Duluth by the Arial Lift Bridge. On one
side Lake Superior, on the other the harbor. Emil lives
about halfway down the Point. It is May 1st. May Day.
We are in the sauna in the basement listening to the ball
game. Emil says, "We need it hot today." 180. 185. Even
190. We lay on our backs on the benches with our feet
on the ceiling. I think of red, red lobsters in the pot. It's
out the door, up the basement stairs, over the dune, and
to Lake Superior. Emil plunges in and swims out. I get
ankle deep. There are still massive chunks of ice on the
lake.

Emil climbs on a blue-white ice slab, jumps up and
down, saying, "A new record!!"
"Emil," I say," it's May 1, two o'clock in the
afternoon. You're standing on an iceberg." He gets a look
on his face. I know that Jesus must have walked on the
water because I saw Emil do it as he came back to the
shore.

The Cosmic Sauna

Earth, air, fire, and water—this is my true
experience. "Sumalina Boyka"—"Finnish Boy"—as
my grandmother used to say. Changing in the small,

drafty outer rooms, hanging clothes on a nail or leaving
them in a pile on a chair not meant for sitting. Sitting
naked on the cedar or pine bench. Feeding the fire. The
bucket with cold water, sometimes water from the pump,
sometimes lake water with minnows still swimming in
it. A dipper full poured on the rocks. Another poured
over your head to cool you down. Feeling the heat open
you. The pungent smell of cedar and sweat and smoke.
Soaping up. Using a washcloth to wipe down. Watching
the thermometer inch upwards. The satisfying taste of a
beer, or water, as you sit on the bench.

This is good. This is the sanctification of the eternal,
sacred elements. Wood becomes fire. Fire generates
heat. Water becomes steam. Steam invites sweat. Sweat
becomes cleansing. Heat is replaced by cold. Cold closes
pores and ends sweating. Cold invites hot again. Earth,
air, fire, and water. Yes, I affirm it. I relish it. I seek it
out. I celebrate it as my true heritage and belief.

One of the joys of the list story is the freedom of telling from any point of view—first, second, third—and in any tense, past, present, or future. In this version of the sauna cycle, the first segment is told in the first-person but is "universal" in tone. By "universal," I mean the images are more poetic than personal. The second segment is in the third person, while the next three are in first person and are based on direct experience. The final segment is back to the first-person universal.

I cannot think of another narrative form that is so open and malleable. Whether you use it as the research and development mechanism for other plot forms, or use it to present material, it provides a wonderful balance between utility and freedom to experiment that can produce great stories.

Exercises

1. In developing a list story, let us begin once again with deciding what story we want to tell. As tempting as it is to do a list about the pets we have had or the cars we have driven, for the purposes of learning the form, let's pick a folk or fairy tale. Think about the elements of the tale. Who is the hero or heroine? Where and when does it take place? What happens? You may want to jot those elements down just to have as a reference.

Now take up those three-by-five cards and make the first decision: how many segments will this list have? We know it will need at least four to meet the requirements of the formula, but for the sake of this exercise, let's say that you are going to use seven, and, while we're at it, we'll give a nod to the hero's journey.

On the first card, put the image that sets the theme for this story. This may be an invocation of time and/or place. It may be a description of the hero or heroine, or something told from his or her point of view. Here is the tricky part: this image not only announces the theme for the list but must also be the invitation for the journey. To do so, make your first vignette capture our attention.

On the second card, let's work out a joke or a humorous statement that offers the audience members reassurance that they can follow this story. It might be fun to make a joke commenting on the eagerness or the resistance of the hero or heroine to the call to adventure.

On the third card, introduce the person or animal that is the hero or heroine's helper. This segment can be in the first- or third-person point of view. If in the first person, create it from the hero or heroine's or the helper's point of view. One of the decisions you'll need to make is now is who telling the story—the hero or heroine, the helpers, the opposition, or a neutral third party—and for the sake of learning the form, once you decide who that is, use their point of view in repeated segments of the list. Even though the list form is a segmented story with multiple options for time and point of view, it will create a stronger story if you are consistent about who is telling the story.

On the fourth card, identify the most important challenge that the hero or heroine must face.

On the fifth card, let's describe the moment of triumph when the hero or heroine achieves what has to be done.

The sixth card is our next-to-the-last card, the emotional-payoff card. On this card, put what the essence of the story is about and why it matters to the hero or heroine, or to the narrator, or to the audience for that matter. You will want to find a way of saying this metaphorically or by demonstrating the point through action rather than saying "this is the moral of the story."

On the last card, we want to return to our larger theme, and, if we are true to the hero's journey model, to the place the story began as well. It is worth the effort to find the compelling or lyrical image that complements what you used on the first card. Perhaps it is a variation on that first image; perhaps it is another version of the time or place that was described.

Now that you have filled out the cards, write or tell the story end to end. In what ways does it let us understand the folk or fairy tale in a new light?

2. Having worked a folk or fairy tale to learn the form, try this again with a personal story. Pick a theme. Here is the moment to tell the story of the lessons learned in team sports or the accidents you have had. Tell the story of your best or worst meals, of the places you have lived, or the seasons of the year in your town.

Use one card for each item on the list. As an example, if you are doing a list story about funerals you have been to, on the first card, write "funerals" (the general theme). On the second card, write what's funny about funerals. On the third card, write whatever you want to say next. Then go back and add to each card your notes about the central image, action or emotion for that item on the list.

Now that you have the bare bones of the story, flesh it out end to end. Tell it or have someone else read it. What did that person like? What questions does he or she have? What did the person want to hear more about or read more details about? Does that mean you need shorter or longer vignettes, or a shorter or longer list?

Once again, the value of the list narrative is that it lets us take a lot of material and streamline it to get to the essentials. If you are not sure what the story is, using this exercise will help you sort it out, even if you eventually choose another narrative form to present it to an audience.

CHAPTER ELEVEN

FALL BACK

"Time is the longest distance between two places."
Tennessee Williams

The Regression Plot

Formula: D-C-B-A (End)
Focus: Time progression
Book or movie: Martin Amis' *Time's Arrow*
                 Memento

The regression is a plot form in which we begin at one moment and slip backward in time. There is only one direction, and it is a journey to a place somewhere before the moment with which we started the story. In effect, we begin at the end and go back to the beginning. There is no coming full circle, as in a flashback.

An example of this plot form is the movie *Memento*, where the hero has suffered a brain injury and cannot make new memories. Because he cannot remember what just happened, he uses Polaroid pictures to identify whom he has met and tattoos notes to himself on his body as he tries to find his wife's killer. The story is told in segments, each one set in an earlier time than the one it follows. Each segment ends with the first thing you saw in the preceding segment. Each raises questions about what is happening and the meaning of what you have already seen. Is the best friend to be trusted? Is he even a friend? As you go back in time, you discover that the actual story is not quite what you thought it was, and, like the hero, you are faced with a mystery in which the nature or meaning of the clues shifts with each segment.

When done well, the regression plot form can be very satisfying for both the creator and the audience. It can present emotional complexity and invite deep participation in understanding the story. Moreover, the regression plot offers an elegant opportunity to have an audience consider a puzzle and fit the pieces together. This sounds more challenging than it actually is. As storyteller and NPR commentator Kevin Kling says in one of his stories, "Don't be afraid. I'm not."

Since the audience puzzles out what is happening, the real beauty of this plot form is not what happens but in how you reveal what happens. These stories often are philosophically or psychologically loaded. They can be full of nuanced description and emotional invitations that reward the audience for making the journey. They thrive on the suggestive and descriptive details that unveil the story scene by scene.

The image of peeling away the layers of the onion, of each layer revealing another, is an apt metaphor for this kind of story. Let's take a closer look at the form by peeling away the layers of *Jack*.

> *Jack wonders, "What makes for happiness?" as he sits in his silk bathrobe. He thought he had been carefree but now he realizes that even though he has everything he could have dared dream of, he is more miserable than he has ever been. He has lived the life of a wealthy man for many years now, but his sleep is troubled. He tosses and turns with dreams of death. In each dream, the face of the Giant appears, getting ever closer, filling space, screaming insults and accusations. Jack runs, but the Giant is always close, and getting closer each night. Those massive hands are always grasping for him. That angry mouth — the gnashing teeth yellow with decay and flecked with spittle — grows larger with each night's vision. He should have realized at once that only tragedy would follow his boldness.*
>
> *Was it really necessary to go back for the singing harp? Oh, she was a cruel enchantress, all melody and charm in the Giant's hands. Who would not want to have her when he touched her taut strings? For all her charm, she played his too eager-emotions as surely as . . . oh, she sang all right. Sang a warning to the Giant. Sang a lament and protest even while Jack tried to still her long enough to slip out of the door.*
>
> *Why couldn't he have been satisfied with the goose that laid the golden eggs? When he carried it home, it sat*

in the nest in the corner, contentedly producing twenty-two carats a day. Hadn't the race to escape the Giant with the bird in hand, avoiding the rain of blows, and that cursed refrain — "Fe, fi, fo, fum, I smell the blood of an Englishman; be he alive or be he dead, I'll grind his bones to make my bread!!" — been terrifying enough? For that matter, even that first bag of gold would have been enough to feed his mother and himself for the rest of his life. How much gold did he need for happiness?

Or was it the thrill of climbing the dizzy heights of the beanstalk that made him reckless? What a sight it was, to feel the muscles gripping the green vine, and to lean out, look down, and see the farm fields stretching to the horizon in every direction. He remembers the thrill of waking up that first morning to see the beanstalk ascending. Had he even thought of whether it would hold his weight? No, it was just the fact of it, the thin spiral of green like a line from earth to Heaven, calling him to adventure. After all, wasn't it a miracle that when he looked up from his bed, there was anything there at all? They could just as easily not have been "magic" anything.

His mother had doubted the power of those beans. Jack hadn't. They were the key to his fortune, but what sense had it made at the time? No one who thought for a minute about economic value would have traded beans, even so-called magic beans, for a cow! Did he have the sense he was born with? Had they not grown, would he have understood how foolish he had been? His mother had been clear about his obligation. Take the cow to market and sell it. And he had, or at least he had started to.

Was he always doomed to want something for nothing? To want just a little more than he deserved? But in those days, there was nothing in the cupboard, and he had to do something. Why hadn't he gotten a job instead of lying around the house wondering about life? A lazy boy, Jack had spent his childhood dreaming his life away with tales of adventure and daring. Could his mother have been right? Couldn't he do anything right?

In this version of *Jack,* the focus is on the emotional consequence of action. We begin at the end, after he returns home, and ask the one question that belies the very notion of "happily ever after." Then we revisit each of our segments and raise the questions that are unspoken in the traditional story. In this version, Jack becomes a prime candidate for therapy, filled with doubt, and what little humor there is in the story comes from standing the "happily ever after" cliché on its head.

Of course, the regression plot is not limited to unhappy or humorless stories. As with all of these plot forms, it can be used in humor as well. One of the best examples of that application is *No News,* a story that I first heard told by Barbara Freeman and Connie Reagan, who are known as The Folktellers, at the National Storytelling Festival in Jonesborough, Tennessee. For those who are not familiar with the story, I'll summarize it. It begins with the simple question, "Did anything happen while I was gone?" and goes on to reveal that "nothing" happened, that there is "no news," except for the fact the dog died. And how did the dog die? Well, from eating the burnt flesh of the horse that was killed when the barn burned. And how did the barn burn? The barn was set ablaze by the spark of a candle from the wake of the mother-in-law who passed on. And when did the mother-in-law pass on? Oh, she died after the wife ran away with the gardener. But like they said, there was no news.

Since the basis of this plot form is the going backward in time, the first assumption you might make is that you can begin your story's construction by taking the standard narrative and just reversing it. Unfortunately, that approach doesn't guarantee the story will work. Because standard narrative is focused on what comes next, the approach usually fails to provide the necessary connections that the regressive plot form requires. It is not enough to know where you are going. You have to begin your story construction from the audience's point of view, and develop the plot in such a way that they can follow it as you move back through time.

With a regression plot, you must begin by providing a compelling point of entry. It is in the inviting of the audience into the story that the first, and often the most difficult, hurdle is found. The first image must set the tone and may present the essential mystery that the rest of the story will explain. With each successive image or layer, the audience must hear the story on two levels: what is happening now, and how this explains or connects to what already has been revealed.

For my example of this plot form, I turn once more to a ghost story. Over the years, I have enjoyed hearing and collecting these stories. The process of creating them has led me to use a wide variety of plot forms to achieve the nuances of unease that a ghost story should contain. Here is one in which the regressive plot both drives the story to its conclusion and supports the elements that create suspense.

Sleeping with Her Ghost

Though he stood at the basin for a long time soaking his hands in warm water, they remained numb. He glanced at the photograph on the dresser next to postcards in the black envelope and knew his hands had lost feeling from the moment he had picked it up.

Earlier that evening, he had shared a cup of coffee with the younger sister of his high-school girlfriend. As she got up to leave, she had put the picture in his hand. "Take it," she said. "I've stopped trying to understand why she did it." It felt as cold in his hand as late-winter ice, weightless and brittle.

It was supposed to be just catching up on old times. They had casually chatted about his life and hers. She was married now, selling real estate and really doing quite well. He was still traveling. His new photography exhibit was well received and all that. What they didn't say, what they tiptoed around, unsure of how to acknowledge, was her sister's death. But finally it could not be avoided.

"It's funny," he said, "sometimes I can't quite remember what she looked like. And when I think that I've actually forgotten her face, I'll have a dream, and she'll be in it."

"This will help you", the sister said, pulling a picture of the dead sister out of her wallet. It was the last one, taken a few days before she died.

He stared at the open face with its sad eyes set wide

apart, the small mouth holding not a smile so much as a forced grin. He couldn't really tell what color her hair was in this black-and-white snapshot, but it was cut short, with curls, exactly as she had worn it when they had slept together.

No, wait a minute. That couldn't be right. He had never slept with his high-school girlfriend. He had slept with . . .

He looked at the picture a second time. It certainly was her or someone who looked very much like her. But his high-school girlfriend didn't have a twin. His high-school girlfriend had been dead for five years, and he had slept with this woman just a few days ago.

"You know it was suicide," the sister said, letting the unspoken have voice.

But he was lost to the sister's words. Instead his mind drifted back to the other woman, the one in . . . no, the one suggested by the photograph. Back to the morning after he had slept with her. Back to the moment when she had wrapped her arms around his naked waist as they looked out the window of her cabin. They were watching the deer appear and disappear, moving gracefully through the early-morning sun, retreating further into the stands of white birch and the dark beyond. In the rose light of dawn, the deer cast no shadows.

What had she said? The deer crossing in and out of shadows were like life—always present but not always visible. She had laughed and stood on tiptoe to put her head on his shoulder. He could feel the softness of her flesh pressing close, but curiously, it was without warmth. He put his arms back around her as if the awkward embrace could ward off the chill.

"You can keep the postcards," she said for a second time.

The night before, they had made love. The night before, she had brought out a box of postcards for him to look at. "Take as many as you want," she said. "I have no use for them." He wanted to take them all but politely

selected a dozen rare ones that he arranged on top of her
naked body as a tour of pleasures yet to come. Between
kisses and caresses, they looked at each in turn, and
she put them into the black envelope, saying, "Here's
something to remember me." Then she kissed him a
long, passionate kiss and said that where she was going,
no postcards ever came back with the words "having a
wonderful time, wish you were here."

The circumstance of their meeting was curious but
certainly not a wonderful time. When he first saw the car,
it hardly seemed that anyone could have lived through the
wreck. You could follow the skid marks from the edge of
the highway. The car must have been traveling fast when
it hit the guardrail, because it seemed to have run along
the top for some distance before the rail gave way and the
car rolled down the embankment. It came to rest wheels
up, the grill wedged between two rocks in the creek. A
thin rainbow of oil shone in the light as it flowed towards
Lake Superior while a trail of glass, bits of chrome, and
broken branches led back towards the highway.

He thought she was dead. She was lying on a flat rock
next to the car, her skirt up around her waist. When he
slid down the bank, with a shower of pebbles, she opened
her blue-gray eyes and said, "I wondered if you would
come by."

Me? Did he know her? She looked so familiar with
her open face, the eyes set wide apart, the small mouth,
but he couldn't place her. Where had he seen her before?
Was she the girl talking with the locals in some North
Shore bar that had caught his eye? The woman in front of
him at the check-out line he had casually flirted with? The
silent waitress pouring coffee in some cafe who would not
laugh at his jokes?

"Yes, you, or somebody very much like you."

"Is this your car?"

"Was. Say, could you give me a ride home? I don't
think this car has enough gas to make it."

Driving along that road, he used to wonder what

happened when his high-school girlfriend made that final drive those many years ago. One day, he stopped wondering and read the police report. After that, he could imagine it for himself.

There were no streetlights on that stretch of highway—it was two-lane blacktop with loose gravel shoulders. A steady rain was falling. The dashboard lights were dimmed, the speedometer creeping upward: forty, fifty, fifty-five. Somewhere along the way, she shut off the windshield wipers. Somewhere along the way, she turned off the headlights. Sixty, sixty-five. Turned up the radio. It was not set on any station in particular, perhaps one arriving on a transcontinental skip, jumbles of static between bursts of all-night jazz or some gospel preacher calling her home to Jesus. She must have driven the pedal to the mat. The car shuddered on the wet pavement—sixty-five, seventy. The trees crowded the road—seventy-five, seventy-six, seventy-eight. The wheel caught the edge of the pavement. The car jerked. She let go. The car wiggled sideways on the wet grass beside the road, caught the guardrail with the left side of the bumper, and climbed the steel. Sparks flew as it made the fifty-foot slide along the rail.

Maybe she looked in the rearview mirror to see what comes after the fear and saw herself. The engine roars. The tires spin in the rain, grabbing air, gravel, and branches of the hillside shrubbery as the car turns over. The sound of bending metal fills the night and collapses from its own weight. Broken branches. Broken glass. The windshield crumples as the roof of the car slides down the stony bank towards the rushing water. Stones scrape. The rearview mirror gouges a furrow before it breaks. When it comes to rest, steam rises from the hot engine. Dashboard lights go out. The radio is silent. There is just the dark and the sound of the rain. The blood mixed with the water.

Structuring the Transitions

The most difficult challenge of the regressive plot is making the backward movement as smooth and seamless as possible. You want to avoid the overuse of phrases like "before that" and "earlier," which ultimately put the audience off. In this story, as an example, the transitions are based on descriptive images and factual statements. I use phrases that help shift the frame of reference: "but he was lost to the sister," "when he saw the car," and a rhetorical question, "What happened on that final drive?" Then, within each layer, there is a chosen tone or central image that is the foundation of that section. The photograph of the sister, the image of the deer in the shadows, the postcards, the dialogue at the scene of the accident, or the description of the final drive—all move us through the story and serve as an anchor for their respective sections.

The regression narrative is not used often enough to be familiar to most audiences. In a written form, the luxury of being able to go back to read something again helps anchor the reader in the particular moments of the story. In an oral narrative, the task must be accomplished by the clarity of imagery and the emotional arc.

With careful choices, you can easily move the audience's understanding of the story forward as the plot progression moves backward in time. To make a transition from one segment of the story to another clear, it may be easiest to begin by identifying the central image of each segment of the story. How will you set it up? What does it flow from, and what does it lead to? How does it take the audience into the action or meaning of the story?

The key is to make sure each layer of image is located within a specific time and place. These can be geographical. They can be emotional. They can be chronological, though a strict adherence to a time progression may feel strained. Choose details that invite the audience deeper into the story. In some stories, it is the use of a sense (smell, taste, sound, etc.) that serves both as the anchor of a section and the bridge from one moment to another.

What is implied also can provide a path from one segment to another. You should allow for implication in the story to suggest what the audience should fill in. As an example, in my story, I never say that the woman in the story is the ghost of the high-school girlfriend. It is implied by the repetition of the phrase "her open face, the eyes set wide apart, the small mouth" to describe the photograph and the accident scene. The description at the end is a description of the high-school girlfriend's suicide and also the accident where he meets the girl. I want there to be enough similarity and ambiguity about what is happening to let the audience members arrive at their own conclusion about what the story is about and, in the process, internalize the story for themselves.

Exercises

To construct a regression narrative, let us begin by taking the three-by-five cards and laying out the progression of a story of our choice. What is the beginning? What comes next? Each critical image or action is put on a card all the way through to the end. OK, now you just start from the last card and work your way back. Well, sort of. You do want to rearrange the order so the last card will be the probable starting point for the story. "Probable" is the right word.

The first thing you need to do after reordering the cards is decide whether the last image is the starting point or whether there is some other, more compelling place to begin. If it is not the last card, you may want to throw it out, and move the card that will be the strongest invitation into the story into the starting point.

Now, you need to mark those image and action cards that are essential to the story. Don't throw the other ones away just yet, and be sure that as you move the story from a particular point in time to an earlier one, you are moving from one clear image or action to another.

Since the transitions are critical to the regression story, create a separate card for each transition and place them between the appropriate narrative segments. As I said earlier in the chapter, look for clear and inviting images or turns of phrase to keep from repeatedly saying "before that" or "earlier."

Now, write or tell the story. Once you have done so, examine how well the movement back in time has worked. If need be, strengthen your transitions by adding to or shifting their imagery. Then, rewrite or retell your story.

CHAPTER TWELVE

TWO TRAINS RUNNING

"To illustrate one thing by its resemblance to another, has been always the most popular and efficacious art of instruction."
Samuel Johnson

The Parallel Plot

Formula: (A-C-E)
             (B-D-F) End
Focus: Point of view
Book or movie: Günter Grass' *The Flounder*
                Chicago (the movie)

The parallel plot is a form for those who love metaphor or are just plain undecided about their point of view. It is a form in which segments of two (or more) related, or even seemingly unrelated, story lines are woven together. The parallel plot often is used to present the differing points of view of characters within the same story.

Each story line provides a framework for understanding the other. The meaning of the tale comes from the union of the multiple story lines in the audience's mind. The form can be as clumsy and awkward as a mixed metaphor in a sentence. It also can be as elegant as DNA, two strands spiraling and informing a whole, when it is well constructed. In those stories in which a synergy of the diverse elements is present, the whole is more than the sum of its parts.

In the early stages of constructing parallel plots, it is helpful to choose relatively simple story lines. Care must be taken not to choose plot lines that are so divergent or unrelated that they cannot be understood as being linked in some way. It might be difficult, for example, for an audience to see the parallels between the point of view of a cat or dog with that of a teakettle, instead of the more promising pairing of a cat or dog and its master.

Once you have worked out the essential points of view of each side of the parallel, you can begin to work out the mechanisms of

why and when you move from one segment to another. As is the
case with the regression plot form, the transitions from one segment
to another are critical. In the regression plot, the transitions help
make it clear to the audience when something happens. In the
parallel plot, the transitions help make the "who" or the "why"
clear. For example, in the movie version of *Chicago*, all the song-and-
dance numbers are representations of the imagination of the central
character and quite separate from—but triggered by—events in the
external narrative story.

If, as an example, one plot line is the internal, first-person voice
of a character speaking to emotion and thought, and the other is
an external, third-person narrator describing the actions, how does
going from one perspective to the other move the full story forward?
Do you want to highlight the contrasts or inconsistencies between
what is felt or thought, and what is done? Do you want to use the
third-person point of view to show how other characters react to the
main character, and reserve the internal monologue for what cannot
be seen or known except by the main character?

My example of parallel plotting can be told in several ways.
When I first developed it, the story was told from a heterosexual
perspective based on two experiences that I had at about the same
time. The experiences struck me as different in context but very
similar in outcome. After telling it a number of times, I had a gay
man point out that this story also spoke to his experience. At that
point, I modified the tale in such a way that it can be told using
any combination of gender pairings to suit your sexual preference
depending on how you use the pronouns.

Music Lessons

When he/she first saw him/her sitting at the audition,
playing a musical saw, he/she wanted to laugh. There was
a charm in his/her technique, a confidence that stifled the
laugh, and, listening carefully, he/she began to appreciate
the ethereal quality of the sounds emerging from that
union of a violin bow and an industrial tool.

"I'm amazed, really." "You should try it." "Me?"
"Yes, why don't you come over to my place sometime, and
I'll give you a lesson."

When she/he first met him/her, all the signs were right. She/he was attracted to the slender frame, the dark eyes, and sensuous mouth. She/he couldn't help but notice that she/he had very good hands, well cared for, but then everything about him/her said elegance. It was an elegance that she/he could appreciate.

"A musician, I should have guessed. The bassoon, not a common instrument to play. We should have coffee some time, and you can tell me about how you came to play the bassoon." "Yes", she/he said, "I'd like that."

When he/she walked around to the back door of the old duplex as instructed, a feeling of panic rose and was quickly put aside. The neighborhood was "iffy," and the stairs to the apartment looked positively unsafe. This would be an adventure. Inside, the kitchen was beset with unwashed dishes and cluttered shelves, but what he/she noticed was the yellow table in the center of the room on which there was a bottle of Jack Daniel's and two glasses.

"Did you bring a saw?" "Yes, I've got a 36-inch Craftsman, just like you said on the phone." "All right, they've got the best tone of the commercial saws. Just sit down in this chair, spread your legs, and I'll slap that saw in place." "I'm not sure why, but I'm a little nervous about this." "Well, can I pour you a little one to calm you down before we learn the positions?" "Yes, I could use a sip of courage now."

When she/he approached the restaurant table, it was set with white linen and a little vase of fresh flowers. This was the kind of place where the coffee came in real china cups and the waiters looked like they all had post-graduate degrees in attitude. Not quite the informal meeting in an upscale coffeehouse that she/he had envisioned, but an enthusiastic wave and a gesture to take a seat at the table put him/her at ease.

"Oh, I'm so glad that you could join me." "Well, you promised to tell me your story." "Not all of it, it's much too boring, but certainly enough about the bassoon to make you wish you hadn't asked." "No, I'm sure I'll

be—why don't you proceed, and I'll just practice being
enthralled."

The secret of the musical saw, she/he said, was not in
the strength or speed of bowing the saw's flat edge, but in
maintaining and releasing the tension of the curve.

"You can't hold it too tightly or too loosely." "I'm
not sure I know how to hold on at all." "Here, let me put
my hand on yours, move you around a little to give you a
simple demonstration. Am I leaning in too close?" "No,
it's very comfortable."

The secret to the bassoon, what makes for the
virtuosity of the playing, she/he said, was all in the
control of the position and agility of the tongue.

"Bassoon players must have a very talented tongue."
"Yes, very talented. When the opportunity arises, I'll have
to give you a demonstration." "Yes, I'd like that, uh, to
hear that, I mean." "Oh, is that what you meant?" "Why,
wasn't that what you meant?"

She/he was standing behind him/her, so close that he/
she could feel the weight of his/her body pressed against
his/her shoulders and his/her soft breath in his/her ear
whispering instructions. One set of hands holding the
other, guiding the movement of the bow and saw. The
sounds that emerged began tentatively but took on
confidence as the two of them learned their way. When
they put down the saw, they picked up the glasses, and
drank the bottle empty. They could feel the whiskey burn
like their own desires, all the way down, and held each
other closer in that bare kitchen.

As she/he was walking her/him to the car, she/he
gently placed an arm around her/his shoulder and guided
the yielding body into an embrace. They stepped back
from the street into the doorway of an anonymous office
building. That was the moment, the very moment when
she/he kissed her/him. That was when she/he knew what
had been meant about the secret of the bassoon, for it was
an exceptional kiss. A kiss soft and wild, that felt like she/
he had a humming bird's nectar-tipped wings brushing

her/his waiting lips.

In this example, the corresponding elements of the parallel plot are highlighted by the segment pairings: both couples meet, sit at a table, talk about musical technique, and then engage in physical contact. The separate elements of each story, including the choice of genders and different class status, are consciously chosen to sharpen the audience's ability to follow the sequence. The separate elements also suggest the real subject—the universality of desire that cuts across class or sexual orientation—that remains outside the told story.

The value of a parallel plot is that it lets us compare and contrast two points of view or courses of action. Consider this example in which Jack and the Giant's actions are told as a series of politicized vignettes:

> *Jim the Giant is a high-life, corporate tycoon surrounded by guards wearing Armani suits, a gaggle of yes-men, and corrupt right-wing politicos seeking campaign contributions. He can buy and sell governments at the click of a mouse. All sound and fury, he is prone to pronouncements: "Fe, fi, fo, fum; I smell the blood of a liberal bum. If he's alive, he should be dead, then I'll grind his bones to make my bread." Jim the Giant follows the old rules: buy low, sell high, use the best, throw away the rest. He praises the global free market of cheap labor and lax environmental rules that encourage conspicuous consumption. The Giant knows someone has entered his castle. Where is Security? Can he trust his wife? Since when are her charity functions and prescriptions not enough? Can he trust his mistress? Who has the videotapes of their kinky roleplay? Is she having an affair? Is she cheating on him, the man who took her from a whiny folk singer to a tabloid pop star?*
> *Third World Jack, with his self-taught hacking skills, slides through the shadows and byways of the Infobahn, reading the supposedly encrypted communications that send workers to the unemployment*

line, watching the program trading of global exchanges, hearing the whispered reports of injustice, and he vows revenge. He will speak up for every nameless little man and game-playing geek that has ever dreamt of revenge. Jack comes out of hiding long enough to divert the off-shore accounts through a series of data-laundering ports, and, using anagrams of his name, deposits the funds into the bank accounts of a thousand charities and advocacy groups around the world.

Everywhere Jim the Giant looks, he sees his fortune being dissipated. Here, the gold price fluctuations have cost him millions. There, the poultry futures market has produced an unexpected goose egg. Blinded by anger, Jim the Giant grabs at shadows, his once-comfortable world now full of unplanned disappearances and conspiracies. He trusts no one, and now has no one to turn to. He sees Jack's taunt of being "the Giant killer" come through his private web-cam communication, but who is this Jack? Jim the Giant doesn't know Jack! There is no dossier for Jack. It is as if he had no electronic fingerprint. Yet, there is a man here on the screen, calling himself Jack, holding the Golden Harp, the private key to his power.

Not content with a virtual snatch-and-run, Jack decides to enter the corporate tower to show it can be done, avoiding or distracting the security cameras, disrupting the elevators, leaving a taunt spray-painted on the penthouse wall. All around him, he sees what he does not have and does not want. And yet the temptation to become a Giant prompts him to sit at Jim the Giant's computer and see what little Jack can do. What's this thing called the Golden Harp? Could he crake the code and call its tune?

He strikes yet another blow for the underdog, plotting the ultimate downfall of Mr. Big from his own desk. Days of toying with Jim the Giant pass before Jack returns to the corporate tower, entering the penthouse office. He seizes the Golden Harp, intent on confronting the Big Man. Afterward, he will use the instrument to make

the power structure transparent, naming all the names,
highlighting all the shady connections and illicit deals,
and then making the source code available to all.

   But where is he? Jim the Giant looks closer and sees
his own office. Sees himself sitting at his own desk, turns,
and sees a physical Jack with his PDA-mounted webcam
in hand. It plays out like a scene in some cheap B-movie.
Jim the Giant doesn't think. He reacts, rushing to attack
this interloper Jack, who simply steps aside and lets the
Big Man's momentum carry him over the penthouse
balcony. Down, down the hundred stories, Jim the Giant
sails to towards the uncaring crowd below.

   This story ends with justice and fortune
intertwined—an unhappy end for one and the basis of a
new virtual reality game for the other.

In the parallel plot form, the material does not necessarily have to be arranged tightly. What is crucial is that the audience can hear or read the correspondence between one story line or element and another. They should feel that each story line is clear, distinguishable, and appropriate. The audience should have some sense of investment with each of the story lines. If each of the story lines concerns a separate character—Jack and Jim the Giant, as an example—each character must be fleshed out. The audience should be able to sympathize or at least understand the point of view or actions of each character. If the plots are tracking a single character, the audience should be able to distinguish the difference between internal and external, between thought and expression, and between intention and action.

Parallel plots do not have to reach a conclusion. In most instances, as when we are doing a story from the killer and the police detective's points of view, they probably will. But we could create a powerful story in which the characters never meet except in the mind of the audience members, who can see how they are similar or different. Think about a story in which two characters are faced with a similar problem and make different choices, and we follow how each choice plays out. Think about another story in which two characters share something in common but do not know it, and one character is incidental in the other's world. The possibilities of the parallel plot are unlimited, and the beauty of them is that you can construct several variations to see which best serves your story needs.

We are almost finished with the examination of plot forms. What are the mantras that you should have internalized by now? First, the construction of a narrative is a process of conscious decision-making about how we move from beginning to end and what point of view or emotional tone we want the story to have. Second, it is the details and the transitions that engage the audience. Keeping those in mind, let's go to the last of our plot forms, and see how you can be both inside and outside the story as you tell it.

Exercises

1. Taking the three-by-five cards, lay out the basic narrative progression of a story of your choice. For the purposes of this exercise, I will use *Little Red Riding Hood*, but you can use any folk, fairy, or personal story. Having laid out the basic narrative progression, take a second set of cards and decide which portions of that narrative will be represented by the first of the two story lines. On a third set of cards, you will put the portions of the narrative that will be represented by the second story line. You should now have three sets of cards—one for each of the parallel plots, and one for your original outline of the basic progression to use as a reference. Here are three ways that you could explore the parallel plot:

a. One plot line is Little Red Riding Hood's point of view and the second is Grandma's or the Wolf's.

b. One plot line is the first-person, internal point of view of any one of the characters and the second is the third-person, external view of a narrator.

c. One plot line is in the present tense (either in first or third person) and is focused on actions or emotions, and the second one is told in the past tense (again first or third person), and is focused on the larger impacts, the cultural considerations, or the meaning of the story as it played out over time.

Pick one and write or tell the story using that construction. Once you have completed the writing or telling of that version, pick a second and retell the story using that construction. What are the differences? Was one easier to do than the other? Why?

2. In "a" of the previous exercise, the characters interact with each other. Imagine another version of the same story where the characters do not directly interact, but where we can get the gist of the original story through parallels of behavior, attitude, or emotions. As an example, a version where one plot line is that of someone who sees Little Red Riding Hood picking flowers across the meadow but does not speak with her, and the other is that of a woodsman recounting the story of a wolf in human clothes that he was told by another woodsman. What has to be done to make these parallel but not interactive stories work? How important is it for the audience to know the story that is being referenced?

CHAPTER THIRTEEN

AS I WAS SAYING

"You never really understand a person until you consider things from his point of view."

Harper Lee

The Metaframed Plot

Formula: A–B–(m1)–C–D–(m2)–End
Focus: Point of view
Book or movie: Tom Stoppard's *Rosencrantz & Guildenstern Are Dead*
                Ferris Bueller's Day Off

The metaframed plot may be thought of as the first cousin of the digressive plot. Within the telling of what is usually a straight narrative, the author or performer steps out of the story to speak directly to the audience and comment on the story itself. In the digressive plot, the wandering from the narrative path is incorporated into the story itself. In the metaframed plot, the teller separates himself from the story line, breaking what in theater would be called "the fourth wall" and acknowledges that this is a story and that both the teller and the audience are separate from the narrative content being communicated.

We often arrive at the use of this plot form by chance, or in response to the particular circumstances of telling a story to an audience. Sometimes, a teller begins a story and makes a mistake or realizes that in order to bring audience members up to speed, he must speak directly to them. There is no more useful metanarration in the face of an error or forgotten detail than "there is something you should know." This breaking of the story line often is extemporaneous, especially when used to correct an error, but I'll tell you this: when you use it once, you have to use it again. Otherwise, the audience will feel that the breaking of the story line is not a matter of conscious choice, but the result of an error.

Metaframed narration also is used by many storytellers and

musicians to invite the audience's participation, as when a folksinger comes to the chorus and says to the audience, "Everyone, join in." It is an acknowledgment of the reciprocal bond between the teller and audience. In traditional folk narrations, this often occurs when a teller stops the story at various points to explain local, cultural, or historical references to people who are unfamiliar with the story, or to respond to comments or questions from the audience.

The metanarrated novel as a literary form is fairly common, going back at least as far as Henry Fielding's 1749 publication of *Tom Jones*, a novel in which it seems that the narrator addresses the reader directly in every chapter. It extends through Fitzgerald's *The Great Gatsby* and John Fowles' *The French Lieutenant's Woman*, to the contemporary warnings that the audience should skip over the unpleasant parts of *Lemony Snicket's A Series of Unfortunate Events*. Typically in these works, the author or a character in the story addresses the reader to suggest how the reader ought to feel or act in response to the narrative being presented.

Here is old *Jack* for the last time. I will use brackets to enclose the metaframed text.

> [*This, of course, is one of those old stories that you know or think you know, having heard it as a child. But like most of those children's stories, what you think you know and what the story actually is may not be the same.*] *Jack lived with his mother in a small house on the far edge of town. Poorer than church mice, they were. She sends him to town to sell the family's last cow and he does, but not being too smart, he takes magic beans as payment. Mother is furious, throws the beans out the window, intent on starving them both to death.*
>
> *Overnight, those beans grow up and up, miles into the sky, and in the morning, Jack is out of there, climbing up the beanstalk just like that. Jack arrives in the land of Giants and is amazed that the castles and himself don't just fall out of the clouds. The boy finds himself at the home of the Giant. Knocks on the door. Goes in, gets himself something to eat. [Now, here comes the good part, where the Giant comes home, and sings that little song of*

his. You know it, and you can sing it with me: *"Fee, fi, fo, fum, I smell the blood of an Irishman. Be he alive, or be he dead, I'll grind his bones to bake my bread."* Cheery little ditty, isn't it? Let's sing it again with some feeling, like we're Giants stomping around the house.] Anyhow, Jack is hiding so the Giant doesn't find him. When the Giant gets tired of looking and goes to take a nap, Jack steals a bag of gold. Comes back. Same thing happens again. [Yes, I know you want to do it because we had so much fun the last time—let's all sing the song again. *"Fee, fi, fo, fum, I smell the blood of an Englishman. Be he alive, or be he dead, I'll grind his bones to bake my bread."*] So this time Jack steals the goose that lays the golden eggs.

The boy is starting to enjoy this stealing stuff from the Giant and thinks to himself, *"Why not go back up the beanstalk a third time?"* Yes, he does, and the same thing with the food, hiding, and Giant happens just like it did before. [OK. Here's the last time we sing this song, so any of you shy people who have been wanting to do this but haven't—just join in now, loud and proud. *"Fee, fi, fo, fum, I smell the blood of an Englishman, Irishman, young'un. Be he alive, or be he dead, I'll grind his bones to bake my bread."* Oh, that was good!!] Jack takes the golden harp but this time the Giant isn't really asleep. Now there's going to be some trouble because the Giant chases Jack all around the castle, but Jack is too quick.

Jack slides down the beanstalk like it was a greased pole. He grabs the axe. Wham, bam, thank you, ma'am— the beanstalk is chopped through. The Giant is finished. [So is the story.]

In this version of *Jack*, I did one commentary at the beginning to set a context for the story and then limited the metanarration to engaging the audience in direct participation, inviting them to say the phrase that is probably the best-known part of the story.

The narrative you are telling can be in first, second or third person but the metanarration always is in the first person, addressing the audience directly.

Metanarration can be very useful in working with elements that do not transfer easily to the page, or that require a higher level of awareness to have full effect. Irony, as an example, is predominately a verbal experience and often fails in the written form. Metanarration provides a context for irony that invites the audience to join you in seeing the tension between what is said and what is meant, no matter if the material presented is spoken or written.

My example of a metaframed plot is a performance piece that I did for a number of years that was based on randomly selected quotes from Herman Melville's *Moby-Dick*. It has a fairly high irony quotient and is riddled with direct addresses to the audience. The example below also includes stage directions in brackets and quotes from Melville's novel in darker text.

Moby Dick Tonight!

[Lights up with performer on stage with suitcase and chair. He opens the suitcase, takes out a copy of *Moby-Dick* and reads.]

The first time I read Melville, I was working on an old-school trawler. There in the bowels, I was cutting fish heads and emptying the innards. Hour after hour, the bright slicing knife would enter the soft, white belly and make its way towards the tail, not in anger or sorrow, but in a peculiar rhythm repeated without guilt or pleasure. The smell was so strong, you stopped thinking about it, dared not let your nose remind you of the rot death commands. It would crawl under your apron, under your sweater, under your hair, and sink into the muscle beneath the flesh. You could not scrub it out.

Hmmmm, that's so visceral. Hang on, it gets better.

Sometimes, weeks later when caught in a rain, the smell of the rough soap would be overrun by the smell of the cutting room. In that wet-dog moment, I would be hurled back to the belly of the beast, the clank of the machinery, the harsh lights, and hours standing there up to the ankles of my rubber boots in the guts that were covering the floor. Iridescent bubbles of mucus, translucent sheaths of green or black membranes with veins like colored thread. Sometimes, the eye of a half-digested smaller fish would stare reproachfully through the lining of a stomach.

This was how I paid for my education in the ways of the world. I was hungry for the profit, and in my precious spare hours, I picked up Melville, but did not see the irony of the story before me.

"Call me Ishmael."

Melville begins with a name: Ishmael, the other son of Abraham, the firstborn son, the son not tested with the knife to please a jealous God, the one cheated of his inheritance. But what matter—by choice or circumstance, Ishmael leaves home.

"Call me Ishmael. Some years ago—never mind how long precisely—having little or no money in my purse, and nothing particular to interest me on shore, I thought I would sail about a little and see the watery part of the world."

I went to sea in search of adventure, looking for billowing white sails before the wind, for the creak and groan of the mast and the rigging, and for an old salt bathed in Old Spice. I wanted to feel my sea legs dancing upon the deck.

What I found was the monotony of endless work, cramped quarters, and bad food. A life of salty tears strewn on storm-washed decks. They leave the ship, my water and the ocean's, commingled, sweeping onward before wind and current towards the fondly remembered shore. That great longing informs the wave, curls upon itself, gathers strength, and crashes upon the rocks. Freed from their watery bond, my tears leap into the air to fall upon the much-loved-and-lamented land.

[Take the small bed and pillow out of the suitcase. Put the pillow in place on top of the suitcase.]

In my adventure, in my exile, there were always dreams of the one left behind, standing on the widow's walk, the dock of the bay, watching the glowering clouds

*scud over the slate-gray sea. They wait for the sight of
ships returning home. In the distance a sail appears, a
whaler come to port, but it is not mine. I will not return.*

*The waves rise and fall, rise and fall, a reliable clock
keeping count of our longing. We sleep, my lover and I,
alone. We sleep, my lover and I, with an ocean between
us, listening to that unhurried pendulum of waves' rise
and fall, rise and fall.*

*Bound by circumstance. Bound by Fate. I ask you,
what difference does it make whether I choose this inn to
rest my weary bones or another? This cheap bed shared
with Queequeg or another? After the bundling—after
the breathless wonder of his naked flesh next to mine,
the smell of man and sea, bodily fluids, and sweat—to
wake and dress in his shadow, walk the docks in search
of a ship, to sign on as crew to this ship, the Pequod, or
another? By the time Ahab nailed the gold coin to the
mast for the man who would conjure him Moby Dick, by
the time I, Ishmael, raised my voice with the others for our
common profit, the hunt for the great whale, my Fate was
sealed, the story foretold without my knowing it.*

*Do you want to know what the story really is? A
man fights a whale. The whale wins.*

*And yet there are stories within the story. Invisible
to the naked eye, but as real as the winds filling the sails.
I have told this first story. If that is what you want, the
bare bones of plot, take your leave. But if you want to hear
those other stories that lay beneath the tattoo, beneath the
waves, beneath the dreams dreamt in a seaman's bed, stay.*

*There is too much to tell, so I will content myself
with four who are principal to the tale: Ishmael, the
dispossessed son; Queequeg, the beloved harpooner; Ahab,
the instigator of all that follows, though not the story's
hero; and of course, Moby Dick. Each one bound to the
other, and each given his time upon this stage.*

[Light shift.]

*What is this work we do? Six men in a small boat:
two pairs of rowers sitting fast upon each other, hip to*

hip, shoulder to shoulder as if in a harness, bound to the
work of reach and pull and the tillerman in the stern.
The harpooner stands in the prowl with the instrument
of our purpose, and three more waiting at his feet. For
each harpoon, a tub of coiled rope twelve fathoms long.
All around, open water as far as the eye can see. Behind
us, the ship is close but not close enough to swim to if the
boat should fail, or, worse yet, the whale succeed. Beneath
the water, the great shadows move, rise up, breach. The
spray flies up, followed by the monstrously large, arching
back as the whale surfaces and dives in one motion. We
are on them. Straining our backs against the swell to be
there when the whale comes up, but not so close as to have
it breach beneath the boat.

Queequeg stands in the bow with the harpoon held
high. The slick, gray back of the whale appears, close
enough to let the sharpened blade be launched. Hard and
fast! There! The harpoon strikes. The whale dives, its
great tail splashing the company. The line sings out. As
it does, we pray that the beast will turn, tangling itself,
be forced to rise again before the line plays out, slowing it
long enough for a second harpoon to meet its mark before
it makes another descent. Only a fool would grab the rope,
or tie it to the boat to be pulled into the watery deeps.
Many a fool has done both. Few have lived to regret it.

After, the body floats on gray-green water. If it were
a man, he'd have drowned, for the whale, like men, are
creatures of air swimming in water. We strain at the oars
to bring the dead weight of still-warm flesh to the ship
to be secured snug to the side. This whale is a third the
length of the ship. Three times the length of the whaleboat.
This whale is not Moby Dick.

[Light shift.]

When Queequeg had left the sea, the sea had not left
him. Tattoos bare in the dim chamber of the inn, I thought,
"This other is not man but holy writ," for as I came to
learn his body, the story of his people—their creation,
birth, death—all were marked within as well as on him,

*as surely as the border of a letter marking the bounds of a
word. Every mirror named him as chosen. He was word
made flesh, and his will would be done. In truth, in every
cramped bed of every hold, in every inn, when he slept
alone, he slept with a harpoon held as tenderly as a lover
so that its sharpened blade might take instruction from his
flesh, that his will might be its own — straight and deep
the entry, deep as the sea, deep as memory, deep as Death
itself.*

*On land, he walked on shaky legs, unsure of his step
when the floor did not rise, fall, rise again. My foot was
firm and welcomed land even as I sought to leave it. I
held him even in his unsteady gait, as he held me in the
embrace of men who killed for profit. His was hard work,
not for the faint of heart, and, I soon enough learned,
not for me. For Queequeg, yes, but not for me. I bear no
visible mark of bearing or history, but am marked as sure
as farm fields measured by stone walls, and city lanes
with this door welcoming those with money to spend and
that door welcoming those who would ask God's mercy.
Marked just as sure as Ahab's scar as not of this watery
world, with the sting of whale breath in the open boat,
the fear grip of the rising shadow made monstrously full,
or the baneful eye reproaching the advancing harpoon.
Queequeg will forgive me turning away. But that is to
come. In the days of the hunt on steely, white-capped sea,
it is row or be dammed.*

*After, Queequeg now stands on the slippery
geography of flesh, his feet comfortable astride death.
Washed by bloody waves, he works the harpoon out of the
wound. He licks the blade to taste the life that was, kisses
the steel to reward it for doing his will, then reaches down
to enlarge the cut so the blubber hook might be inserted.
Once it is, those aboard the ship begin to winch the line.
The ship leans towards the whale, further, further until
with a snap, the flesh sunders, and is stripped away in
long sheets until all that remains of the whale is carcass,
organs, and bones. These are cut away to sink beneath the*

*gunmetal waters. What is cut from the bone is winched
onto the deck and the waiting maw of commerce.*
[Return to the chair, pick up the book]
   *"Meanwhile, [Melville reports] the spade man
stands upon a sheet of flesh, perpendicularly
chopping it into pieces. This spade is as sharp as
one can make it. The spade man's feet are shoeless,
the better to grip the whale's slippery geography.
Though his will is strong, the thing he stands on
sometimes slides irresistibly away . . . . Toes are
scarce among veteran blubber room men."*
   [Light shift.]
   *The blubber room is as industrious as can be
arranged in forty feet. The blubber falls through the hatch
from the deck with a wet thud. Seawater and blood splash
the blubber-room men. The smell of accumulated salt,
tar, rot, and sweat mixed in the charcoal smoke permeates
the hold. The light dim, the task singular—cutting flesh,
loading tubs, rendering oil, filling the wooden barrels to
be stored in the hold below—all illuminated by sputtering
lamps consuming the very profit of this enterprise. From
life to slab to slice to boiled sustenance that will light a
thousand, thousand hissing lights of Ishmael's fondly
remembered shore. Such is our love of progress.*
   **"Thoroughly consumed by the hot fire of his
purpose, Ahab in all his thoughts and actions ever
had in view—Moby Dick."**
   [Take handkerchief out of suitcase. Place bed on
the closed suitcase. Run hand across the bed, laying
a red, silk handkerchief over it like a shroud.]
   *He was sitting at the edge of the bed, his whalebone
leg unscrewed beside him, the Captain's black coat and
stovepipe hat hung by the door. He was nothing if not
precise, organized. A place for everything and everything
in its—hmmm, better put as "everything of use." His
weary eyes told no tale but were fixed upon the dream of a
green and gold sea where the great fish play.*
   [Take out a cigar. Smell it. Caress it.]

Often he would polish the harpoon, running his idle hands lovingly over the stiff pole and, with the gentlest of caresses, stroke the blue steel tip. No, sorry, that was Queequeg, not Ahab. Ahab had no love for the harpoon, though it would be the instrument of his vengeance or his destruction. No, when Ahab sat upon the bed, he was like Ulysses lashed to the mast hearing the Siren's call — terror at the prospect of that which was wanted above all else and cannot be had. Moby Dick was that Siren call — the monster that devoured his leg and "unmanned" him, as Melville so tactfully put it. And Ahab personalized it. Had the replacement leg made out of the jawbone of a sperm whale.

[Light the cigar. Savor it.]

All right then: for those who have been napping, let's review. Here we have the story of a magnificent tattooed dark-skinned harpooner, a naive adventurer discovering his sexuality, a mad Captain, and an albino fish. This is supposed to be a classic, which many of us read, or attempted to read, in high school. Let's see the hands of those who read it. How many started it? OK, let's see the hands of those who finished it. I thought so.

Too long? Too hard to work your way through the extraneous stuff? Too confused about who was doing what to whom? You're not the only one who thought that. In fact, the book was that not very well received in its time. Considered a literary mess, it was only after the First World War that it was called a metaphor for our struggle with mechanistic culture, or Melville's critique of Protestant religion. More than one critic has called it an apt demonstration of the search for meaning in a treacherous world. Now, I realize that we could be moving towards the end of a long and thin academic branch here, but stay with me. We're not actually going there. After all, it is a simple story in the end: man fights whale, the whale wins.

[Examine the cigar, take a long, deep inhale and exhale.]

So you're asking yourself, "What is the deal with Ahab already?" For starters, he's been struck by lightning and has a scar that the crew believes runs from head to foot. Got struck and survived. That's strike one. Got chewed up by Moby Dick and spit out. Strike two. Ahab doesn't believe in omens. Dammed near everyone else on the boat does, but not the big A. He really believes the third time's going to be the charm—pardon the metaphoric shift—that it will be a belt-high fastball down the middle that he can hit out of the park.

I met Ahab once. Or rather an Ahab-like personality so intent on the rightness of their cause they could not imagine another possibility. A bag lady—smart, educated, interested in politics. Attended every city council meeting, and plenty of others as well. Got herself appointed once to a Commission on Homelessness. She could have made a difference, but took every opportunity to snatch defeat from the jaws of victory. Even when you wanted to be sympathetic to her point of view, even when you agreed she was right, she'd find a way to turn it back, irritate, and frustrate. I used to imagine that she was really a Ph.D. professor of social behavior conducting a field study on how much people would put up with. I thought if I followed her long enough, I would catch her putting her bags in the trunk of a Mercedes discretely parked in some downtown garage, and she would drive back to the suburbs to write up the day's notes on how to piss people off. That was actually a more comforting thought than the other one: that she, like Ahab, was driven by a burning rage to strike out at everything that offended her, always and just because.

[Open suitcase, place bed and handkerchief inside. Return to the book.]

"From his mighty bulk the whale affords a most congenial theme to enlarge and amplify—would you, you could not encompass him."

The value of symbols is that they mean more than the "this" or "that" they present, and the tricky thing is that

*they often work in ways not intended. A symbol means
what we want it to mean. Melville might have thought
of Moby Dick as the embodiment of Fate, but we are not
bound by his intention. What would Moby Dick be for
you? What is your great obsession, the singularly wanted
beast of dreams and shadows that will cost you more than
an arm and a leg in the end?*

*For me, it is a certain kind of woman who is both
beautiful and a danger to herself as well as any man who
gets involved with her. The second time I read* Moby-
Dick, *it was given to me by a beautiful, dark-haired
junkie who favored Kenzo and Donna Karan. A Jewish-
American princess who became the queen of darkness —
more Lilith than Eve. She was lots of fun, at least at the
beginning. I was Ishmael in search of adventure when I
met her, but I became Ahab tangled in the paralyzing lines
of a singular purpose before the last page was turned.*

*She was newly arrived. I found her an apartment,
a job, a car. She liked her kicks short and sharp. Liked
the designer dresses, shoplifting bikinis she could easily
afford, the fever and the damage done. Liked reckless
sex, binge drinking, disco dancing in the gay bars, white
lines snorted two at a time. Liked wild rides the wrong
direction on one-way streets, shouting and giving out
the slaps, then the tearful reconciliations. I was hardly
pure — I enjoyed drama as much as the next faux hipster.
Every time she offered, whatever she offered, I accepted as
if those acts of indulgence were enough to seal our bond, if
not our fate.*

*I'd come back from the work-a-day world, see her
lying on the bed, her eyes as blank as a TV screen. She'd
turn to the wall, showing me the long curve of pleasure
that ran from her shapely ass to the nape of her neck. It
was as joyful as sighting the elusive white whale. Hard
with desire, I'd slip into bed in search of any tenderness.
The smell of good perfume, incense, and stale Chinese
takeout hung in the room. It was our snug hold on the
stormy seas of wanting.*

"Bring my horse," she'd say, "bring me my pretty pony. Tie him up, baby, tie him up, and let me mount. Oh, the spurs jingle, jangle, baby. The spurs hurt so good. I want to be riding. I'm so happy when I ride."

I rode that horse myself a few times.

Out would come the foil and the hush. Out would come the matches and the spoon. Out would come the tie and then the rush. Out would come the needle and the swoon.

She'd leave the bed long enough to stick classic Sinatra or Ornette Coleman on the stereo. I'd do her first, then take a taste for myself. I knew where she'd been, I said a hundred times, looking at her blood on the hollow tip of panic. I didn't, of course, lying to myself about risk and wanting as jazz filled aimless, lingering hours, drifting the dark waters of some unspoken dream, a tangle of arms and forgetting.

It ended badly, as I knew it must. Coming back to the apartment one cold January day, it was empty. The furniture, dishes, everything—even my clothes—gone without "goodbye" or "so long, sucker." The job quit, the car sold, I embraced a shameful longing for what might have been instead of the sullen fact of what it was. I embraced lethargy, pissed away ambition and any hope of getting on with my life. I wanted to see her again, just to hurt her. Just to plunge my spite-sharpened harpoon into her selfish heart.

I took my recovery in the smoky depths of a waterfront bar to nurse a cold one. A stripper who did things with a beer bottle that gave new meaning to the phrase "it's Miller time" had just left the stage when there was a roll of drums, the crash of a cymbal. The announcer stepped to the microphone: "Ladies and gentlemen, the Club Pequod is proud to present Moby Dick tonight."

[Light shift – harsh white spotlight]

Out of the squid-ink darkness, a man emerged. At least it seemed to be a man. His immense girth was truly a sight to behold. The very air seemed to shudder as he walked, pushed aside by a mountain of white flesh hanging on a bloated face. He filled the stage, his white suit shining in the harsh spotlight, covered with the stains of everything he ate, drank, puked, and spat in the last decade. The lungs sucked air in audible gulps and wheezes, which were amplified through the club PA, until it seemed we were all gasping our last with him. His fingers were swollen around pinkie rings.

Jokes fell from livered lips already dead, smelling as old as last week's bait. From the back of the gloom came a nervous laugh. A voice says, "What's this crap?" The thunderhead of slack flesh at the microphone turned his baneful eye to peer into the deeps and opened the great maw of his mouth, revealing broken teeth.

"Well, you pissant hemorrhage, what did you expect? Dick's the name, symbolism's the game?"

This is how the story ends: one man, Ishmael, is riding a coffin on the open sea. Saved by Queequeg while all around him perish.

But you look confused. Perhaps that is too much, too soon.

Let us enter the moment: Ahab, the once-defeated challenger, has his shining dream of a rematch. Moby Dick—the reigning champion, rising as pale as the moon, pale as bleached bone, a continent of ill will, bad luck, and trouble—offers him one more shot. The harpoon strikes. The black line sings out, but Ahab is not as quick on his feet as he needs to be and is caught on the ropes. Down for the count. Man and beast plunge into the depths. Turn. Breach. Ahab is bound, ensnared—this is not what his rage had foreseen but what Fate decreed: cursed flesh to cursed flesh.

Man fights whale. Whale wins.

The ship, the crew, all who bet on the outcome are lost; everyone bound by the oath of profit to the hunt for this great beast suffers the same defeat. The white whale turns, rises, tangles the lines, and plunges down. The boat is sunk. Every man gone but one alone left to tell the tale.

I, Ishmael, saved by the emergence of the coffin.

Clinging to Queequeg's intended end—the carved, canoe-shaped coffin prepared for his death with biscuits, a flask of water, and a pillow for his head—Ishmael embraced death even as he once embraced Queequeg in the cold bed of the Innkeeper's night or the rough bunk of the Pequod's hold. Even dead, Queequeg opens the path for Ishmael's understanding.

[Light shift. Put cigar in suitcase, Take out dinosaur. Inflate. Stand dinosaur on top of suitcase.]

"What whale is this?"

What? You can't see a connection? They're both very big. They've been around for a long time. So I don't have an inflatable whale, OK? Just think of it the way Roland Barthes would—as a signifier. Geeeezz, do I have to do all the work for you? Why don't you connect the dots? Please, you fill in the blanks.

They ruled the roost. Had their fifteen minutes. Hell, in the grand scale of history, they had at least an hour. When they came into a room, heads turned. They're all gone now. Zip. Finito. They had lavish parties but were poor conversationalists. Hors d'oeuvres hadn't come into fashion; the cocktail wiener hadn't even been invented yet. Without opposable thumbs, they couldn't hold martini glasses. Still, they managed to drink too much and got into fights. Fell into hot tubs full of boiling tar.

[Turn dinosaur over.]

Was it boredom and lack of social skills? I think not. Hunted for their rich oils and malleable bones? That's not the reason they are no more.

They were once like us—the norm. They practiced good citizenship and shared family values. They knew what to expect from life and were content to take what was offered. Their world was the commonplace, the ordinary, and oh, so familiar. And yet, for them, as for so many of us, the familiar is invisible.

Once you're invisible, you might as well be extinct.

[Lights out. End of show. Bow. Then post-show music.]

I should note that there are actually two kinds of metaframed narration in this example. One is the inclusion of the stage directions addressed to you as a reader or to a performer of the piece. In the usual presentation of this story, the audience sees the results of the stage directions, but here you get to read them instead. The other metaframed narration consists of the various direct addresses to the audience, as when the performer says, "Let's see the hands of those who read it. OK, let's see the hands of those who finished it. I thought so."

Before we leave this chapter, let me repeat the fundamental rule of metanarration: You can't do it once. Suppose it arises from a mistake. You forget something or get something in the wrong order and need to make a correction with the audience. If you stop and tell those in the audience that you need to give them some critical piece of information, it telegraphs the fact that you've made an error. Not a good situation. It tends to kick them out of the story and into a mental inquiry: "What else is wrong?" So to move from mistake to metanarration, you have to address them again at some other point. When you make that second comment to the audience, it now is a matter of style and not error. Much better.

I also offer a caution about the use of metanarration that was raised by teacher and storyteller Jane Stenson, who says that it is dangerous as well as insulting to break from a story to explain its meaning when telling to children. I will say that if you are telling a fable, you can choose to articulate a moral at the end of the tale, for that is the nature of the form. But there is no reason to comment on the moral by means of metanarration. It is better to let the story demonstrate the meaning though the action rather than step outside the narrative frame and tell audience members, whatever their age, what the story means or is supposed to mean. Metanarration works best when it can expand our understanding of character, culture, or circumstance, rather than narrow it.

Exercises

1. For the purposes of this exercise, select a folk or fairy tale you want to tell. Using your three-by-five cards, put the essential sequence of the story on the cards. Decide what you want to comment on and at what points in the story you want to address the audience.

Suppose you are working with *Rumpelstiltskin,* and you want to comment on the fact that the father tells the lie that gets the story started but then disappears. OK, the first metanarration will be inserted after the father says that his daughter can spin straw into gold, or, perhaps, after the girl is summoned to the King's palace. Suppose you want to make your second comment about the fact that there is no reason why the girl should want to trust, much less marry, a king who has threatened to kill her if she doesn't complete an impossible task. Your second address will be inserted somewhere around the third spinning episode. Then, you want to finish off the metanarration with a comment about any one of the odd endings of the many variations of the story. Why does the little man stomp his foot into the floor and tear himself in two, as happens in one version, or spank himself with a spoon and run away, as happens in another? Why can't he just accept the fact that he's been beaten at his own game? This will be inserted either just before or just after the end of whatever version you've chosen to tell.

The essential exercise is simply deciding what you want to comment on, what the comment is, and where it needs to go. Remember, if you directly address the audience once, you have to do it at least once more. Having picked your story, decided what you want to comment on, and where you want to comment, write or tell the story.

2. Now that you have tested this process with a folk tale, try it on a personal story. It may be easier or helpful to you if you choose a story with a high humor quotient. This is a plot form that lends itself to irony and the self-deprecating pointing out of assumptions and foibles. Remember the difference between metanarration and digression is that here, we are stepping outside the story to comment on it, whereas in a digression plot, the comments, explanations, and jokes remain inside the story.

CHAPTER FOURTEEN

OTHER CONSIDERATIONS

*"Language is the servant, not the master, and it must
accommodate a vision, not determine it. This requires
simplicity and silence, a reduction of barriers—verbal and
otherwise."*

Ken Feit

Which Plot to Use?

We have come to the end of our survey of plot forms. It should
be understood that all of these basic plot forms can be modified to
meet the specific needs of the writer or teller, or the audience. There
are many instances when it might be appropriate to combine plot
forms, but I caution you about doing so. As the words above the
door in that old folk story *Mr. Fox* so aptly put it: "Be bold, be bold,
but not too bold." The more plot forms combined in a single oral
or written story, the greater the difficulty in shaping a story that
does what a story must do: invite the audience into a world, create
an emotional response, reveal something about imagination or
experience, and convey a meaning.

In order to really understand how each plot form works, I
encourage you to create a variety of stories using the forms we've
examined. The simplest approach is to work and rework a story
you know well, like *Jack and the Beanstalk* or one of your own, and
discover the different possibilities of each plot using the same source
material.

I am not suggesting that each plot form will work equally well
for any particular story you want to tell. Some plot forms—straight
narrative, revelation, flashback, or regression—are best suited to
chronological progression, while the others work best when point
of view dominates. The real value of these narrative forms is not
in their individual strengths or limitations, but in the ability they
give you as a writer or teller to match the needs of your stories to
an appropriate structure. With practice, it will become clear which
plot forms you are comfortable using and which can best meet your

thematic and stylistic interests.

Let me also say that I am not suggesting that it is necessary to begin with the plot when adapting traditional material or developing original stories. It is possible, and perhaps desirable with some material, to begin development of the story with the emotional arc, and then choose an appropriate plot form after you have a sense of the mood you want to create and the direction you wish to take the story.

There also is the need to make the story have a sense of "presence," anchoring it in time, place, and character. Details provide the story's frame of reference. The tools we use to provide details are the common ones: adjectives, adverbs, nouns, and verbs, words that speak to the five senses. It is through the details that we provide the flesh that covers the bones of the plot.

In the World of Story

Often as you begin a particular story, there is a value in setting the scene within a time or place. This is different from the introduction you might make as to why you are telling a particular story. The invitation into the world of the story should be a brief but integral part of the tale, like the first scenes in movies that establish a visual sense of where or when the story happens. Providing a sense of time and place at the beginning of the narrative can help the audience enter the tale. As you move into the heart of the story, you can then choose to strip away some of that detail in favor of plot or character development, or maintain it for a complete worldview.

It may require some practice to find the right level of scene setting. It might be a single sentence. In the traditional folk and fairy tale narratives, the use of the formulaic beginning "once upon a time" is enough to tell audience members that the story is set in the world of imagination. They can suspend their judgment and accept the fact that what happens may be familiar but it is not here or now.

In personal stories, it often is helpful to indicate what year or what culture we are observing. We don't want people in the audience to spend the first few minutes wondering whether they should be skeptical or look for some missing information, but to simply relax and enjoy the ride. Think about the first few sentences of the examples I've offered: "When I was a child living in Hibbing, my family would go to my grandmother's farm on weekends," or "on the outskirts of a village so small it was but a handful of stone houses clinging to the shadow of the mountainside, Guillermo saw a crowd surging towards a rundown church." When this context setting is complete, you can plunge into the story proper, secure in the assumption that the audience has enough information to follow.

Questions to Ask

It is not enough to say that the material must be shaped. In the best of all worlds, every decision to use this or that word represents a choice that supports the whole. All the words count in creating a thing of beauty, and to appreciate how important those choices are, I want to take a little time to look at why particular details and specific choices are made.

The development of an appropriate level of detailing, including the use of silences, can be made on the basis of several considerations. We can ask:

• Does this story enable the audience to *personally identify* with the experience? Who is the hero? Who or what is the story about? Is the experience at the core of the story accessible or foreign to the audience's own experience? Is there a context for interpreting the images of the story? Do they represent the world as the audience sees it? If not, can metaphors and analogies that are more familiar be substituted to help the audience enter the story's sense of time and place?

• What is the *emotional* content? What feelings are highlighted, valued, or encouraged? How does the telling of the story reinforce those feelings? Is there congruence between the emotional arc of the story, the plot that gets us from beginning to end, and the details that put flesh on the bones of the narrative?

• In what ways is the story *descriptive*? Does it create a sense of a particular time and place? How do we know the world in which it takes place? Does it appeal to the senses? Which senses? Does the language or action seem to fit the situation? Does it make it easy to suspend judgment and release our need for logic, or do we have a framework within the material that will help the audience make those leaps?

At the most basic level, does the audience understand the words being used? Does the story use a recognized *vocabulary and style*? Can the audience be expected to know the meanings of the words, especially the vernacular meanings of ethnically or culturally grounded images contained in the story? While this seems so basic as to be obvious, not every audience will share the same language. Differences of age, education, region, race, class, and gender: all suggest a need for the careful examination of the words we use to tell our stories.

• What is the *point of view* of the story? Is it singular or plural, first person or third? Is it told in the present or in the past tense?

• Does the story have a *meaning*? Is it explicit and contained within the framework of the story, or is it arrived at by implication? If it is arrived at by implication, how does the story achieve that result? Does it satisfy—that is to say, does it feel like a complete and well-shaped story? Is it more than the sum of its parts?

• What *values* can we place on this story? Where is the real pleasure of the story located, in the telling or in the hearing? Does it resonate as "true" to the audience? Does it reinforce or model appropriate or accepted cultural values and behaviors? If not, does it provide a way for an audience to accept new or different understandings of the world?

• What are the *aesthetics* of the story? How are the story's structure, style, and themes developed? Is it a familiar story type? Does it have a recognized plot form? How is it presented? Is there a sense of unity, elegance, or beauty within the experience? Does the form limit or open the material? While this may seem obvious, certain story forms—the joke or ghost story, for example—have distinct characteristics. If the story is to be successfully told, those patterns must be recognizable to the audience.

These questions can be asked of every story and should apply regardless of plot form. In answering them for yourself, you can clarify your answers to the fundamental questions that I've asked over and over in classes and workshops: what is the story about, and what does it mean to you? Answering those questions, and using the plot, emotional arc, and details to strengthen and integrate the material makes for a much better story.

Let me illustrate this point with a story that mixes and matches plot form, time, and point of view in service of the meaning. It contains one stage direction in parentheses.

A Roll of the Dice

It was the day after Paul Wellstone's death when he drove up to Duluth to do a workshop. Afterwards, he went to dinner with his pal, Diego Vazquez, and about 8:15 p.m., left for home.

He drove south on I-35. It was a clear, cold night. About 9:30 p.m., just past the Sandstone exit, he swerved to avoid hitting a deer. The car hit the median, bounced back onto the highway, turned upside down, and slid across two lanes of freeway before coming to a stop in the ditch.

He unfastened the seatbelt and got out . . .

No, it wasn't that simple. Let's begin again.

It was the day after Paul Wellstone's death when I drove up to Duluth, and death was on my mind. There had been phone calls back and forth about whether we should even do the Regional Arts Council workshop, but in the end, it was decided that we should, and we did. There were tears and testimonials and a slushy snow outside that matched the mood. Afterwards, I went to dinner with my pal, Diego Vazquez. I had a rare steak and a glass of a robust cabernet. I stopped in the fish shop next to the restaurant and bought smoked salmon at $12 a pound before I got in the car, buckled my seatbelt, and left for the Cities.

I am settled into the drive. At seventy miles an hour, straight south on I-35 from Duluth to Minneapolis, it clocks in just under two and a half hours. On MPR, Leigh Kamman is playing Dexter Gordon, a little hard bop on this clear and cold night. I pass the Sandstone exit when, on the edge of my view, a deer appeared bounding into the car's headlights. I instinctively swerve to the left; the Saab hit the edge of the median. I hear gravel beneath the wheels. The car shudders. I turn the wheel to get me back on the highway and then . . .

Time doesn't slow down. My life doesn't flash before my eyes. I am rolling over, hanging in the seat watching sparks fly beneath the windshield. I look to the right at the headlights coming toward me and think, "I hope no one hits me." Dexter Gordon is still at it, mixed with the sound of metal sliding sideways across two lanes of freeway. I look out the side window and see lights of cars swerving and the embankment coming. The Saab slams to a stop, nose down in the ditch. Newton's Second Law takes hold, and everything in the car is flying forward.

There is acrid smoke inside the car. I'm hanging upside down trying to take the key out of the ignition but can't seem to find the clutch to put the transmission into reverse to accomplish that. I realize my glasses are still on. Good enough.

A guy opens the door, and says, "Get out. The car is on fire."

I brace myself against the roof and unlatch the seatbelt, feel gravity pull me towards the open door. Dexter Gordon finishes a long solo as I reach for the cell phone hanging by its charger cord.

"Leave the cell phone," he says.

"No, I'll need it," I say, climb out, and stand up to see the rear wheels are still spinning.

There is no fire but plenty of smoke. I try moving my body. Everything seems to be OK—no discernible pain, nothing feels broken. Thank God for seatbelts and heavy leather jackets. I try calling 911 and get a busy signal.

A local deputy sheriff pulls up. Seems he was at the gas station by the exit when someone going the other way pulled off to tell him about my problem. He asks me for my driver's license. He asks what happened. When I tell him about the deer, he says, "Never swerve."

The state trooper arrives. He asks for my insurance information. The door is open, and the lights are still on in the Saab. I go to get my bag with the camera and computer out of the back, but the door handle is missing.

Around to the other side of the car, I crawl in and retrieve
the bag, shut off the radio. I will never be able to hear
Dexter Gordon the same way again. I pick up the bag
with the leftover steak from dinner with Diego and the
smoked salmon I had bought. I shoot a couple of Polaroids
to remember this by and head back to the trooper's car.
He asks me what happened and then tells me, "Never
swerve—just hit the deer. It would have caused less
damage." It's much too late for that advice. While we wait
for the tow truck, he listens to a local basketball game.

When the tow truck arrives, the driver attaches a
cable and turns the car over. The one mirror that wasn't
broken is crushed as the Saab rolls over it. Once it is
upright, I reach in and get the keys out. I open the trunk
and take out my suitcase. I don't want to clean the car
out. I just feel like I need to sit down. The right front light
is broken. There are scrape marks down to bare metal
on the hood, and the roof is crushed from the base of the
windshield to the sunroof. I have the urge to get in, start
it up, and see if it will drive, but the trooper says that's
not possible. The tow guy winches it up onto the flat bed,
hands me his card, and takes it away. Good-bye, Saab.

I call my sister. "Hey, can you come pick me up in
Hinkley?"

The trooper gives me a ride to Tobie's, a popular
restaurant about halfway between Duluth and
Minneapolis known for its gigantic sweet rolls. He goes
over to the usual table to have coffee with the other cops
who are sitting there on their break. He tells them what
happened. They all say, "Don't swerve," and laugh like
this happens every day. I suppose for them it might, but
I head into the bar, ask for a Scotch, and swallow it in a
single gulp. Man, that one felt justified. About an hour
later, my sister arrives. I find myself alternately thinking
how dammed lucky I am and irritated at the things I
didn't get out of the car before it was towed: the garage-
door opener, parking-garage key card, cell-phone charger.
I think about what comes next: filing an insurance claim,

getting a rental car, going back to the junkyard, and recovering the stuff I left. But that is for tomorrow. Right now, I want to sleep.

(Teller makes clicking sound with tongue and teeth.) *A roll of the dice will not abolish chance. The most beautiful sound in the world is the sound of possibility as the dice clatter in your hand. Open it up, and they fly out, each cube rotating freely, catching the light and then . . .*

7:30 a.m. Sunday morning. I wake up. Let me say that again, for those words are sweet to hear: I wake up on the morning of my 55th birthday. Double nickels. It is good to be alive.

This story is totally factual and in telling it, I realized the specifics of the accident often are a shock to the audience. I decided to recount the accident twice. The first time, I do so in the third person with a minimum of factual information. Then, I go through it again in the first person with the emotional elements in place. This allows the audience to actually "hear" the story, and lets me explore the relationship of the fact of the story—the accident—with the meaning of the story, which is "a roll of the dice will not abolish chance." As Ruth Sawyer says, "To be able to create a story, to make it live during the moment of telling, to arouse emotions—wonder, laughter, joy, amazement—this is the only goal a storyteller may have." To do so, the choices we make must not be arbitrary or random.

When chosen with care, refined, and tested until one has a sense of the right words and the right order, our stories invite the audience to dwell in them and provide the context for hearing what it means to be human.

CHAPTER FIFTEEN

HAPPILY EVER AFTER

*"Our profane stories speak extemporaneously from the moment,
from personal experience and understanding, from error and
mistake, from a windfall picked up after a storm.
These ordinary stories are good, bad, or indifferent teachers,
but at their core uncommon treasure boxes of the human mind
and mirrors of its soulful life."*
Gioia Timpanelli

In the end, the creation of stories comes down to a willingness
to be open to the very possibility of stories. We must trust our own
imagination and powers of reflection. We must consciously decide
to tell a story and to structure it. We must want to pick up a pen
or speak up. By doing these things, we create stories that educate,
entertain, and enchant, and we continue a tradition that goes all the
way back to our beginnings.

Being open to the possibilities of stories is no easy matter. We
live in a culture in which the ordinary is discounted, while the
sensational and tawdry are extolled. There is always a temptation
to deny the power of our experience, to believe that our day-to-day
lives count for little and that we must "juice" the stories up to make
them more attractive. I will argue against any effort to sensationalize
them to meet some transitory cultural expectation of what a story
should be. When I look at the stories that I tell that are the most
truthful, the most meaningful, the most satisfactory, I see that they
are often the small and quiet stories about ordinary life.

This decision to embrace the commonplace, which is really
a decision to honor the sacred within the profane, is crucial. In
teaching storytelling, I have observed that the hardest thing for most
students to understand is that our lives and personal experiences are
something extraordinary and magical, worthy of sharing with one
another. As I said, we must first recognize the story and then own
it, so that those stories may become, as Gioia Timpanelli says, an
"uncommon treasure box."

The plot material I have covered can help make your personal stories inviting and the meanings of your stories clear for your audiences. But the first step, the crucial step, is in recognizing the "once upon a time" within the context of your own life. Once you open yourself to the possibility of stories, they are plentiful and transformational. They may be found everywhere. Indeed, they come to you at every turn, and there is a great pleasure in telling them.

Not all our stories are funny, or easy to tell. Not every story is easy to hear or meaningful for us at this particular moment. One of the great powers of stories is that over the course of time, they can become life affirming.

As I said at the beginning, I must begin with the premise that every story is true, even if it is not factual. For the sake of truth and the meaning of the story, every story we choose to tell deserves to be told well. Say the words, write the words, and let the story flourish. It is my hope that you have a lifetime of stories to tell and enjoy a lifetime of pleasure in telling them.

APPENDIX A

Some Additional Exercises

Here are some story-development exercises that I have found to be very helpful in both in the classroom and while creating my own work. They may seem rudimentary or familiar to some of you, but if you have not tried one of these lately, it will be worth the time and effort in light of our considerations of the plot forms.

A Matrix for Plotting Hero Stories

Here is a way to graph the elements of a story from your experience or your imagination using Campbell's journey-of-the-hero formula. Fill in the information matrix by identifying the plot elements and key images that will be developed into a story.

Along one edge of a sheet of paper, identify what the story will be about. As an example, these four topics have been used successfully in classrooms and workshops with students of all ages: accidents, work, play, or food. While any topic can be used, each of these has consistently produced good stories, both humorous and serious, and each is a topic about which most people have strong feelings or memories. For the purposes of this exercise, let's use food as the subject of the story.

Along the other edge of the page, I am going to list some questions that must be answered to develop the story. By filling in the answers to each question, I can create a blueprint for the story.

Questions	Answers/Food Story
Who is the hero?	An old Polish gardener
Is there a companion? (the helper)	His dog, Oscar Meyer
Who is the antagonist? (the opposition)	A giant cucumber
Where? (describe place, landscape)	A large city with backyard gardens and alleys.
When? (time of day, season, year)	The summer

What must be done?	Stop the monster "cuke"
How is it accomplished?	With a polka band
What is the invitation? (How does it begin?)	A news report on the properties of radioactive water
What is exchanged?	Pickles for water
What are the challenges? (How many?)	Three
Challenge One?	Make room for the cucumber
Challenge Two?	The cucumber escapes
Challenge Three?	Confronting the "cuke"
What is the triumph? (What happens?)	Strike up the band
Where is the return? (What is the reward?)	Hot dogs at the ball game

Using these elements, I could flesh out a rather silly children's story in which an old gardener is worried because his cucumbers are not doing well. His dog alerts him to a news report that suggests radioactive water helps plants grow. He then trades a jar of his prize-winning pickles for a few gallons of nuclear wastewater that he uses on his plants. The cucumbers seem to thrive, growing and faintly glowing at night. He has to move other plants out of the way. One day, a rapidly growing cucumber breaks out of the garden, crushing cars, growing ever larger as it heads downtown. Bullets won't stop it. The army is useless. His dog reminds the gardener about the plant's love of the polka music the man played while he worked in the garden. The municipal polka band is called in, and while they play, the cucumber dances to its death in a field of farm plows and wood chippers. All that's left is a huge mountain of chopped cucumber. The mayor rewards the old gardener with a trip to the ballpark, where they have hot dogs. The old gardener thinks he recognizes the green, glowing relish that comes with his hot dog as the remnants of the nuclear cucumber.

Variations of this Exercise

The following exercises can provide you with variations of the traditional journey-of-the-hero formula.

Most stories can be told many different ways. One choice is whether to be serious or humorous. In addition to looking at the serious or humorous aspects of a topic, you may want to explore variations on a theme based on these considerations:
- A version in which the journey is made alone.
- A version with a companion of the opposite sex.
- A version in which the challenge is one of physical strength or courage.
- A version in which the challenge is intellectual or spiritual.
- A version in which the hero is not recognized upon his or her return.

The question of whose point of view is being supported is critical to understanding the meaning of a story. When traditional folk and fairy tales are usually told by an omniscient narrator, the third-person voice imparts the suggestion of neutrality. It allows the teller to include a wide array of characters and action in the tale.

In a first-person narrative, you cannot know any more than what that person knows or feels at that point in the story. This is especially true if you are telling it in the present tense. We seldom use the problematic second person—the "you"—because of the inherent difficulty of having the audience understand and emotionally identify with the "you" being addressed.

Yet, each of these is a valid choice for framing the information we give the audience members and the ways in which they will understand the story. What happens when you change the point of view? Try the following:
- Tell the story in the first person (using "I").
- Tell a story in the most difficult of voices, the second person (using "you"). Who is the "you" being addressed? Is it the companion? The opposition? Someone who knows the narrator but is not central to the story? Is it the internal voice of the narrator addressing someone as "you"? How do we recognize ourselves as that "you"?

• Tell the story from the point of view of an animal or object that is integral to the story but not one of the principal characters.

• Have two people create stories around the same topic and plot line, one told from the point of view of the hero and the other from that of the antagonist. Have each person tell his or her story. Where are the stories in agreement? What actions, motives, emotions would be selected or whose worldview would you choose to create a third-person version of the story?

A Life Matrix

Here is an exercise that has worked very well in helping adults develop stories from meditations on their own attitudes and experiences. This kind of review serves two purposes. First, it gives you the opportunity to discover how your worldview has changed over time. Second, by looking at specific subject areas, story material can emerge from the contrasts or consistencies that are identified. As this exercise requires you to consider your experiences over a number of years, it is not suitable for use by kindergarteners through tenth-grade students, though high-school seniors and juniors might be able to use it. Along the vertical edge of a piece of paper mark off five or ten year intervals from your birth to the present moment:

Age	5	10	15	20	25	30	present

Some people begin this exercise believing that their lives have not changed much from one decade to another and choose ten-year intervals. The difficulty is that most of us experience significant changes in the first twenty years of our lives, so I'd suggest using five-year intervals through age thirty even if you switch over to ten-year intervals afterwards. Give yourself plenty of room for the exercise, and don't be afraid to leave blank spots or to go back over the inventory more than once.

Along the top horizontal edge of the matrix are some topics that include both basic biographical information and key assumptions we have about the world. As you fill in the matrix segments, you can develop points of entry for stories. Those topics are:

- Who you were at that time (role)
- Where you were (location/cultural context)
- When (historical context)
- What you did (activities)
- How you felt (attitudes, sense impressions)
- Why you did that (motives)

That matrix would look like this:

	Who you were / your role...	Where you were / your location...	What you did...	How you felt / emotions	Why you did that / motives
Age 5					
Age 10					
Age 15					
Age 20					
Age 25					

Below is another topic list that you could select a number of items from for a second version of this exercise that is focused on experiences. In this instance, you would do an experience matrix for any age.

- What home meant
- What work meant
- What play meant
- What learning meant
- What adventure meant
- What sex meant
- What secrets meant
- What death meant
- What God/religion meant
- What politics meant

When it is combined with the previous list, it will look like this:

At age 10	Who you were / your role...	Where you were / your location...	What you did...	How you felt / emotions	Why you did that / motives
Home					
Play					
Work					
Fear					
God					
Death					
Love					
Sex					
Happiness					

If you want to create the basis for a catalog of your life, you can do a separate matrix for each interval year.

Fill in the prompts with specific images or incidents from your life as best you can. In some instances, the responses will be vague, sometimes just a word, or you will leave a box blank. Do not be concerned about this. Move on. The objective of this exercise is to give you raw material and lots of it. You can always go back and fill in the blanks. Let me also caution you to not look for the motives for doing or feeling something in this exercise. Look for an image and the feeling attached to it. Once you have identified an image, you can plumb the depths after, but not during, raw data collection.

You might also look to see if there are clusters of activity, periods when you underwent significant changes, or certain areas where there are patterns, especially with prompts like learning, work, or sex, that illuminate your landscape. Often, we can create useful fictions based not on the specifics of our lives but on the patterns of how we have responded to similar situations at different times.

In order to expand the images presented in the matrices, here are three exercises that can give you ways of using the information you have outlined:

• Using the experience matrix, select one item and tell a story about a first experience. It could be a first date or a first job, or the first time you experienced a death in the family. Describe the circumstances and feelings it evoked. Tell it in the present tense as if it were happening now. Do not try to burden this version with the weight of fact or hindsight, but focus instead on the moment, on the raw action of what happens next and what you are feeling in that moment. Give yourself permission to imagine the "what if" as well as explore the "what then."

• Tell that story in the past tense, as a memory with all the sense of longing, regret, or satisfaction that time brings. Concentrate on the development of a meaning of the story. Crucial to this second stage of development is the realization that the ultimate meaning, or truth, of the story may be independent of the facts. Do not be afraid to let go of individual pieces of the story in order to create a sense of the whole. The meaning may not reside in every detail, but in particular details. What is fundamental to the story and the meaning of it? Remember, the tailor must cut away some of the cloth in order to make the suit fit.

• Tell a story in which you contrast your childhood and adult views about a topic. How do those perspectives change? How do you reflect those differences in the point of view or time frame of the story? One choice is to tell the story in the first person, comparing the child's vision with that of the adult's, or as a parallel-plot story set in two time periods. Another choice is to simply use the omniscient, third-person perspective to describe the views the character had as a child and as an adult. Is one point of view or way of telling the story more appealing to you than the other? Why?

Keys to Childhood

Many of us overlook the wealth of stories that come out of

ordinary childhood experiences. We tend to see how we grew up as obvious and not unique. While members of the same peer group may have had similar upbringings, each generation has particular experiences—including games, toys, and how time is spent—that make it distinct from other generations. Here are some exercises designed to explore some memories of childhood:

• **Describe your favorite toy.** When did you get it? Do you still have it? If not, what happened to it?

• **Describe the games you liked to play.** Were they group efforts, or did you play alone? Who else was in the group? What was their relationship to you?

• **Describe the best gift you ever received.** Who gave it to you?

• **Describe the best gift you ever gave.** Who did you give it to?

• **Describe your imaginary or invisible friend(s)** Who were they? When did they come into your life? When did they go? What did you do with them?

• **Describe your secret places, the spots no adults went to or knew about.** Where were they? Why were they secret? What did you do when you were there? How did you feel when you were there?

• **Describe the objects of power (lucky marbles, a baseball bat, a doll, etc.) you used or came into contact with in your childhood.**

• **Describe the people of mystery and adventure in your life.** Were they relatives, teachers, strangers, etc.? When did they arrive in your life? What happened after they left?

Do the exercises above with an eye towards seeing the story possibilities from your childhood. Look for the points where imagination and wonder are present. There is a tendency on the part of adults to look at these questions as therapy, to read our image of a secret place or people of mystery as emotional issues to be overcome or resolved rather than as gifts or adventures. If they are or become therapy questions for you, I encourage you to explore them with a counselor.

In the book I wrote with Elizabeth Ellis, *Inviting the Wolf In: Thinking about Difficult Stories*, we talk at length about the relationship of memory and story construction, and how to handle the issues that come up. For the purpose of the exercises below, I encourage you to try to enter into the spirit of play and wonder that childhood held, before growing up and our disappointments and suffering narrowed our perceptions of the magical in the world.

• **Tell a story in which something magical happens**. Do not try to define what magic is—simply allow the improbable, the impossible, the wholly unexpected to appear, and then tell what the result of that appearance was.

• **Tell a story in which you apply your childhood view of the world to your adult life.** What would it be like to have a power object now, or to be able to play with invisible friends?

Exercises for Developing Detail

These are simple exercises that can help you develop a story's details. Each focuses on a particular aspect of the shaping process.

• **What is expressive?** Create a story from the point of view of an object (coffee pot, bowl of cereal, radio, etc.) in which the audience learns the object's identity and functions through descriptions of sensation and action.

• **What is "objective"?** Select an event such as your first kiss, a fight, or an accident that involved a person with whom you have or had a strong emotional connection. Describe the event and the emotions it evoked in the first person.

Now tell a second version as the other person would tell it in the first person, with a focus on his or her responses to the incident. Finally, tell a version as a supposedly objective narrator would tell it in the third person, based on a series of factual statements describing the event. No first-person emotions, no ownership of the actions. Compare the three. Which resonates as true?

Now, select one of the three versions and re-tell it, concentrating on *what was not said*. Focus on the way in which you can establish point of view by discrete choices, by deciding to include or exclude material. Here, the attention to the use of adjectives and adverbs, to words that color and characterize others, will provide a reliable way of indicating what is or is not being said.

• **What is suggested?** Tell about an experience of play, travel, or food, and focus on details that demonstrate a sense of time and place. It should not be an account in which action takes precedence, but an impressionistic one focused on a sense of presence.

Then tell another version of that story in which the descriptions of scenes are "as if in a dream" -- timeless, symbolic of the actions and feelings you have for the experience you are describing. Here is an instance to really give yourself permission to explore and imagine. Do not try to make conscious connections but draw images, feelings, and actions from your inner life, from the unconscious or semi-conscious strata of your mind, from the wide world of cultural references. The urge to have a dream make literal sense is powerful. What happens when you resist that urge in favor of letting the inner world of imagination manifest itself without the constraint of having to be logical or ordered? This free association of images and feelings is what we do in our dreams. The question is can you recreate it on the page or in the moment of telling?

Postcard Exercises

Here are some exercises with postcards or photographs that you can use to create plot variations by using what a physicist might call "a random order in a fixed set of variables." Because these exercises are based on chance, these exercises can produce frustration. However, this exercise can help you find creative points of entry into a tale.

• Randomly select a dozen photographs or postcards of people and places. Then shuffle them and lay them face down. Without looking at the images, select one. This will be the *end* of the story. Select another. This will be the *beginning*. Tell a story that will take you from the beginning to the end.

• Get a group together and take turns having everyone select two postcards from a set of randomly assembled postcards. Give each person a few minutes to prepare a story based on the cards he or she chose as the beginning and the end, and then have each person tell his or her story. Everyone should try to connect his or her story with the one that was told by the preceding person. After each telling, the teller should put his or her cards back into the set.

Shuffle the images and have each person select a second pair. If a person draws a card that was used in the previous round, that person should use it in the same way that it was used before. By this I mean, if the card was used to represent a particular character or situation, you should find a way to blend that character or situation into your story. This will require additional adjusting and cross-referencing story lines. Now tell each of the stories in turn, beginning with the last person who told in the first round.

• After assembling a set of ten randomly selected photographs or postcards, create a story and assign a portion of that story's narrative to each image. Each image will have two characteristics: one is physical (a sense of person, place, work, etc.) and one is emotional. Shuffle the images, and lay the photos down one at a time. Tell the story by responding to each image as it appears, incorporating the physical and emotional elements of each image. This is often a difficult exercise for individuals or groups because you are responding to the images in the order they are revealed. It works best if you think of the story you're telling as a sting-of-pearls plot form.

• Select ten related photos or postcards. (As an example, I once created a set of images by shooting Polaroid photographs of *The Thin Man*, with Dick Powell and Myrna Loy, when it was shown on TV. Each image was a black and white variation of a television screen, which created a dream-like series of slightly blurred pictures.) Shuffle the set, and lay the images down one at a time. They can be a mix of people, places, and things. Tell a story based on the progression, using each image as the prompt for the worldview, or emotional or psychological state, of the characters in the story. The images do not need to be directly connected with the spoken or written text, but must reference it. After you have gone through the ten images, shuffle them again. Tell another story based on the next progression as it appears. How does the order of images influence what you tell?

The value of these shuffle-and-tell exercises is that they encourage improvisation and letting go of the notion that there is only one right way to tell a story. There are many ways to explore a story. Some are more satisfying than others, but each can give us insight into both ourselves as creators of stories and the range of possibilities within stories.

APPENDIX B

NOTES ON THE STORIES

The Rake
Page 36
 This story, based on an actual incident from my childhood, is the first ghost story I created and was first told in a performance at the Elveum Museum in Madison, Wisconsin, in 1979.

The Knife
Page 46
 The core of the story was developed from the "Keys to Childhood" exercise included in this book and was told publicly for the first time at the Minnesota Friends of the Library *Chautauqua* series in 1980.

Smoking
Page 58
 I developed this story in school residencies from 1980 through 1982 and told it as part of the *Amen Koyhote* story cycle in the summer of 1982. The digressions on trouble and waiting for the phone to ring were added during a stint of school residencies in 1986, when two junior-high teachers complained that the story did not have a "strong enough moral focus."

David
Page 68
 This story combines two unrelated events into one story: David Daarst's death in September of 1969, and an extended period of socializing with Bill McCarthy that took place earlier that same year. It was first told in a BAD JAZZ performance with Michael Sommers and Kevin Kling at our 1988 Halloween show at the Walker Art Center in Minneapolis, Minnesota.

The Rabbit
Page 79
 This story has been told in two versions. The one included here

is actually a small part of a much longer story about an incident at summer camp where the boy in the story goes out in a canoe at night and finds a drowned body. Both were crafted in the mid-1980s, when I was especially interested in creating contemporary ghost stories.

Pablito Bueno
Page 86

The seed for this story came from a story-development exercise at a Jennifer Munro workshop in 1992, during which I developed the story from a photograph. This version was told as an improvised story at Balls Cabaret in Minneapolis, Minnesota, the same year.

Making Chili
Page 91

This story was an improvisation on a theme first told at a Wild Onion Storytelling Festival workshop in Chicago, Illinois, in 1992. I have continued to tell it as an improvised string-of-pearls story with three to seven segments.

Sauna Cycle
Page 106

This story has been told in many improvisations in various combinations since it was first told at FinnFest in Minneapolis and at the Iron Range Interpretative Center in Chisolm, Minnesota, in 1983. The individual segments included here were developed between 1981 and 2000.

Sleeping with Her Ghost
Page 117

This story was based on two events from my stint as the Humanities Scholar in Residence at Northern Minnesota in 1981. It was first told as a ghost story using a traditional narrative at the Toronto Storytelling Festival in 1984, and then in its current regression narrative form at the Wild Onion Storytelling Festival in Chicago in 1992.

Music Lessons
Page 124

The parallel-plot version was first told at a Northern Writers' Conference at the University of Wisconsin -Eau Claire in 1987, and the mixed-pronoun version was first told at the 4th Annual Storyfest in Grand Rapids, Minnesota, in 1990.

Moby Dick Tonight!
Page 135

I created the first version of this story in 1988 for In the Heart of Beast Puppet & Mask Theatre's *Experimental Studio* series. The text used here is one of the variations I used for the MN Fringe Festival in 2009 and the Indianapolis Fringe Theater in 2010.

A Roll of the Dice
Page 153

This story was first told as an improvisation at a Washington Storyteller's Theater performance in November 2002, four days after the accident happened. I have told it in numerous public performances since then and am still working on the language and form of this one.

BIBLIOGRAPHY OF BOOKS
REFERENCED IN TEXT
(Arranged by Chapter)

Introduction

Bruno Bettelheim
The Uses of Enchantment
Publisher: Vintage (May 11, 2010)
ISBN-10: 0307739635
ISBN-13: 978-0307739636

Chapter One

Kendall Haven
Story Proof: The Science Behind the Startling Power of Story
Publisher: Libraries Unlimited (2007)
ISBN-13: 978-1591585466

Walter Ong
Orality and Literacy
Publisher: Routledge; 2nd edition (July 21, 2002)
ISBN-10: 0415281296
ISBN-13: 978-0415281294

Chapter Two

Robert Bly
Iron John
Publisher: Da Capo Press (July 27, 2004)
ISBN-10: 0306813769
ISBN-13: 978-0306813764

Joseph Campbell
The Hero with a Thousand Faces
Publisher: Princeton University Press; 2nd edition (March 1, 1972)
ISBN-10: 0691017840
ISBN-13: 978-0691017846

Joseph Campbell (With Bill Moyers)
The Power of Myth
Publisher: Anchor (June 1, 1991)
ISBN-10: 0385418868
ISBN-13: 978-0385418867

James Hillman
Archetypal Psychology
Publisher: Spring Publications, Inc.; 3rd edition (November 1, 2004)
ISBN-10: 0882145797
ISBN-13: 978-0882145792

Carl Jung
Four Archetypes: Mother/Rebirth/Spirit/Trickster
Publisher: Princeton University Press (October 25, 2010)
ISBN-10: 0691150494
ISBN-13: 978-0691150499

Carol S. Pearson
Awakening the Heroes Within: Twelve Archetypes to Help Us Find Ourselves and Transform Our World
Publisher: Harper One; 1St Edition (July 19, 1991)
ISBN-10: 0062506781
ISBN-13: 978-0062506788

Chapter Three

Sandra Dolby Stahl
Literary Folkloristics and the Personal Narrative
Publisher: Trickster Press (October 15, 2008)
ISBN-10: 0915305488
ISBN-13: 978-0915305483

Chapter Five

Ruth Sawyer
The Way of the Storyteller

Publisher: Penguin (Non-Classics) (January 27, 1977)
ISBN-10: 0140044361
ISBN-13: 978-0140044362

Chapter Eleven

Kevin Kling
The Dog Says How
Publisher: Borealis Books; 1 edition (October 1, 2007)
ISBN-10: 0873515994
ISBN-13: 978-0873515993

Chapter Fourteen

Brown, Barbara & Thomas Ninkovich
The Family Reunion Handbook
Publisher: Reunion Research (1992)
ISBN-10: 0961047038
ISBN-13: 978-0961047030

RECOMMENDED READING

John Gardner
The Art of Fiction
Publisher: Vintage (June 4, 1991)
ISBN-10: 0679734031
ISBN-13: 978-0679734031

David Isay
Listening is an Act of Love: A Celebration of American Life from the StoryCorps Project
Publisher: Penguin Press HC, (November 8, 2007)
ISBN-10: 1615554815
ISBN-13: 978-1615554812

Joseph Martin (editor)
Foolish Wisdom: Stories, Activities, and Reflections from Ken Feit, I.F. (Itinerant Fool)
Publisher: Resource Publications (January 1990)
ISBN-10: 0893901741
ISBN-13: 978-0893901745

Studs Terkel
Working: People Talk About What They Do All Day and How They Feel About What They Do
Publisher: The New Press (February 28, 1997)
ISBN-10: 1565843428
ISBN-13: 978-1565843424